The Parent's Success Guide™ to Managing a Household

Edited by H. Dismore

D1378462

WILEY

Wiley Publishing, Inc.

The Parent's Success Guide™ to Managing a Household

Published by
Wiley Publishing, Inc.
111 River St.
Hoboken, NJ 07030-5774
www.wiley.com

For general information on our other products and services or to obtain technical support, please contact our Customer Care Department within the U.S. at 800-762-2974, outside the U.S. at 317-572-3993, or fax 317-572-4002.

Wiley also publishes its books in a variety of electronic formats. Some content that appears in print may not be available in electronic books.

Library of Congress Control Number: 2003114881

ISBN: 0-7645-5926-5

Manufactured in the United States of America

10 9 8 7 6 5 4 3 2

1V/RZ/RS/QT/IN

WILEY

About the Authors

Ro Sila has been a writer and editor since 1974, specializing in business and self-improvement issues. She is the author of *CliffsNotes Creating a Budget.*

Janet Sobeskey is the Home Design and Lifestyle Editor for *Woman's Day* magazine and appears frequently on radio and television shows to talk about household maintenance, organization, and decorating. She is the author of *Household Hints For Dummies.*

Heather Dismore is a freelance writer who coauthored *Low Carb Dieting For Dummies* books. She edited this book.

Publisher's Acknowledgements

Some of the people who helped bring this book to market include the following:

Editor: Tere Drenth

Acquisitions Editors: Holly Gastineau-Grimes, Joyce Pepple

Technical Reviewer: Della Baker, PhD

Cover Photo: © Getty Images

Illustrator: Brent Pallas, Ternion Design

Interior Design: Kathie S. Schnorr

Table of Contents

☺ ☻ ☹ ☺ ☺ ☹ ☺ ☺ ☹ ☺ ☺ ☹ ☺ ☺ ☹ ☺ ☺ ☹ ☺

Table of Contents

☺ ☹ ☹ ☺ ☺ ☹ ☺ ☹ ☹ ☺ ☹ ☹ ☺ ☹ ☹ ☺ ☺ ☹ ☹ ☺

Table of Contents

Part 1

Figuring Out Your Finances

L ike it or not, you deal with money everyday, especially if you're managing a household. Everyone makes and spends money, but some people manage to pay their debts, save, and invest better than others do. The difference is in their money-management skills. You're not born with these skills; you develop them. And improvement comes with practice.

In this part, you examine the current state of your finances, set some goals for yourself, and set up a plan to reach them. You also track your spending and set up a budget. It's pretty painless, and the rewards are enormous.

Chapter 1

What Are You Worth and Where Do You Want to Go?

In This Chapter

☺ Looking at your current financial picture

☺ Setting smart goals

☺ Setting a time line for reaching those goals

Whether you're in Manhattan, Montana, or Mozambique, many maps you refer to have a "You are here" arrow, pinpointing your current location. Why? Because you can't get to where you want to be if you don't know where you are right now.

One tool that helps you get where you want to be financially is a *budget,* a listing of the income you expect and another list of how you want to save and spend that income. Chapters 2 through 7 walk you through the budgeting process, from tracking your spending to creating a budget to investing. However, before you begin budgeting, you need to see where you are (or, in more formal terms, determine your current financial worth) and you have to decide where you want to go (or, set your financial goals). This chapter shows you how to do both.

First Things First: Using This Book

This book is part of a series called *The Parent's Success Guide.* Its main purpose is to help you, a busy, multitasking mom (or dad!), make some positive changes in your life as a parent — in a minimum amount of time.

Brought to you by the makers of the world-famous *For Dummies* series, this book provides straightforward advice, hands-on information, and helpful, practical tips — all of it on, about, and for being a smart parent. And this book does so with warmth, encouragement, and gentleness — as a trusted friend would do.

This book isn't meant to be read from front to back, so you don't have to read the entire book to understand what's going on. Just go to the chapter or section that interests you. Keep an eye out for text in italics, which indicates a new term and a nearby definition — no need to spend time hunting through a glossary.

While reading this book, you'll see these icons sprinkled here and there:

 This icon points out advice that saves time, requires less effort, achieves a quick result, or helps make a task easier.

 This icon signifies information that's important to keep in mind.

 This icon alerts you to areas of caution or danger — negative information you need to be aware of.

If you'd like more comprehensive information about a particular subject covered in this book, you may want to pick up a copy of the books from Wiley Publishing covering the same topic. This book consists primarily of text compiled from

❀ *CliffsNotes Creating a Budget*

❀ *Household Hints For Dummies*

Figuring Out What You're Worth

Think of your *financial worth* as cash in the form of salary savings, checking accounts, and anything else that has value. Here's a quick list of questions to get you thinking about what your financial worth may be:

❀ How much money do you have in bank, savings & loan, or credit union accounts? Do you have a money market account? Certificates of deposit? A Christmas Club account?

❀ For the purposes of figuring your financial worth, include all *liquid assets*, or items of value that you can readily turn into cash.

❀ What other items of value do you own, such as the house you live in (and potentially another one you own and rent out to others), vehicles (land, water, *or* air!), furniture, artwork, jewelry, and other valuable items (like stamps, coins, or antiques)?

☺ ☻ ☹ ☺ ☺ ☹ ☺ ☺ ☹ ☺ ☺ ☹ ☺ ☺ ☹ ☺ ☺ ☺ ☺ ☹ ☺

❁ How else do you have money invested? Think about stocks, bonds, mutual funds, retirement funds, life insurance, and other investments.

By evaluating the items in the three preceding bullets, you may find that you can make them serve your purposes better by *liquidating* them (converting them into cash) and using that money to pay debt or other expenses.

After considering the items that may be worth something financially, you're ready to calculate your financial worth in Table 1-1.

Table 1-1 My Net Worth As Of _____

Item of Value	Value in Dollars
Cash	
Checking account(s)	_____
Savings account(s)	_____
Money market account(s)	_____
Certificate(s) of deposit	_____
Other	_____
Stocks, Bonds, and Mutual Funds	
Stocks	_____
Bonds	_____
Mutual funds	_____
Commodities	_____
Securities	_____
Options	_____
Other	_____
Retirement Funds	
IRA(s) or Keogh(s)	_____
401(k)	_____
Company pension plan	_____

continued

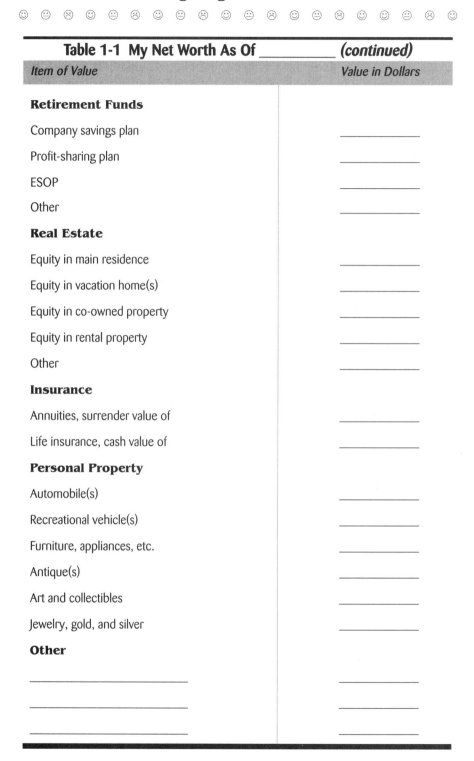

Table 1-1 My Net Worth As Of _____ (continued)

Item of Value	Value in Dollars
Retirement Funds	
Company savings plan	_____
Profit-sharing plan	_____
ESOP	_____
Other	_____
Real Estate	
Equity in main residence	_____
Equity in vacation home(s)	_____
Equity in co-owned property	_____
Equity in rental property	_____
Other	_____
Insurance	
Annuities, surrender value of	_____
Life insurance, cash value of	_____
Personal Property	
Automobile(s)	_____
Recreational vehicle(s)	_____
Furniture, appliances, etc.	_____
Antique(s)	_____
Art and collectibles	_____
Jewelry, gold, and silver	_____
Other	
_____	_____
_____	_____
_____	_____

 As you remember other assets, return to this worksheet and enter their values, adding more lines as necessary.

Setting Financial Goals

Setting financial goals — that is, envisioning a better financial situation for yourself in the coming months and years — is more than just filling in a worksheet with a dollar amount. It's a way to ensure that you'll reach your dreams by taking small steps along the way.

 One reason some individuals and families have a hard time setting goals is that Americans generally don't think of money in the long-term, but think of it in terms of monthly payments. When you buy something that you don't really need because it costs "only" $30 a month, you're ignoring the total cost, which may be many hundreds or thousands of dollars after you've paid it off.

To make goals easier to think about and establish, divide them into short-term, mid-term, and long-term goals. The next three sections can help.

Short-term goals

You can set short-term goals for as soon as next week or as far away as next year. These goals may include paying for a vacation, buying a new stereo, or being able to attend your brother's wedding on the other side of the country.

Fill in your own short-term goals in Table 1-2. (The first three items are examples to help get you started.)

Table 1-2 My Short-Term Goals

Goal	Amount	Goal Date
Save for spring vacation	_____	_____
Buy Christmas presents with cash	_____	_____
Pay my share of parents' anniversary party	_____	_____
_____	_____	_____
_____	_____	_____

continued

☺ ☺ ☹ ☺ ☺ ☹ ☺ ☺ ☹ ☺ ☺ ☹ ☺ ☺ ☹ ☺ ☺ ☺ ☹ ☺

Table 1-2 My Short-Term Goals *(continued)*

Goal	Amount	Goal Date

Mid-term goals

Mid-term goals are usually defined as one- to five-year goals. These goals might include going back to school or buying a car. Mid-term goals can also be stepping stones to long-term goals: If buying a home is a long-term goal, saving for a down payment may be a mid-term goal.

Fill in your own mid-term goals in Table 1-3. (The first two items are examples to help get you started.)

Table 1-3 My Mid-Term Goals

Goal	Amount	Goal Date
Save to buy a newer car		
Start fund for house down payment		

Long-term goals

Your long-term goals are five-year or longer plans. These goals are for long-term plans such as buying a house, paying for your children's college education, and retiring.

In Table 1-4, write your own long-term goals and the dates by which you hope to achieve them. And be sure to go back to Tables 1-2 and 1-3 and add any short-term or mid-term goals that will help you meet your long-term ones. (The first two items are examples to help get you started.)

☺ ☹ ☹ ☺ ☹ ☹ ☺ ☹ ☹ ☺ ☹ ☹ ☺ ☹ ☹ ☺ ☺ ☹ ☹ ☺

Table 1-4 My Long-Term Goals

Goal	Amount	Goal Date
Pay for daughter's college education	_____	_____
Retire at age 55	_____	_____
_____	_____	_____
_____	_____	_____
_____	_____	_____
_____	_____	_____

Part 1: Figuring Out Your Finances

☺ ☻ ☹ ☺ ☻ ☹ ☺ ☻ ☹ ☺ ☻ ☹ ☺ ☻ ☹ ☺ ☺ ☻ ☹ ☺

Chapter 2

A Dollar Here, a Dollar There: Tracking Your Spending

If you're like most people, your annual income doesn't seem like a bad salary, but when it arrives as a biweekly paycheck — after taxes, insurance, dues, and other expenses are taken out — it seems pretty paltry. You may find yourself spending each paycheck to pay your bills and cover miscellaneous expenses and wondering where all that money went. And you certainly don't have anything left over to save for a rainy day, much less for college expenses or a new house.

This chapter helps you answer that nagging question: "Where's all my money going?" You may, in the end, be surprised how your morning cup of cappuccino, weekly Chinese takeout, and monthly cable bill add up to big expenses throughout the year.

Keeping a Spending Diary

Keeping a spending diary helps you determine how you're spending your money on a day-to-day basis. For your diary, use a small notebook that fits in your pocket or purse. Carry it everywhere. Attach a pen or pencil so you have no excuse for not writing down every purchase you make. Every day, every cent, for at least a month. This includes everything from a cup of coffee to your rent or mortgage check.

On each new page, write the day and date. Record your purchases whether you spent cash, wrote a check, used a credit card, or added to a tab that you may have at a coffee house or bar. At the end of each day, total your expenses.

 To make this exercise even more useful, divide the amount of your biweekly paycheck by 14 to find out your daily income, write that amount on each day's page, and at the end of the day figure out whether you spent more than you made that day by subtracting your daily expenses from your daily income.

 The easier your system for tracking your finances, the more likely you are to do it.

You can keep your diary in one of two ways:

❇ Use two columns: one for the amount and one for a description. Table 2-1 shows this sort of table.

Table 2-1 My Spending Diary for (Today's Date)

Amount	Description
$1.50	Coffee at Joe's
$0.50	Newspaper from vending machine
$7.50	Lunch at deli
$1.00	Candy bar
$39.48	Gas for the truck
$33.88	Groceries

❇ Decide on a few wide categories, such as food, transportation, utilities, household, and miscellaneous. Write a key in the front or back of your notebook so that you can keep track of the items within each category. For example, under food you can use G for groceries, C for coffee, R for restaurant meals, and S for snacks.

Table 2-2 shows an example of this type of spending diary. The codes for Transportation are P for parking and G for gasoline; the miscellaneous codes are C for clothing and N for newspapers.

Table 2-2 My Spending Diary for (Today's Date)

Food	Transportation	Miscellaneous
R $10.50	P $5.25	C $39.00
S $2.50	G $39.48	N $2.75
G $33.88		

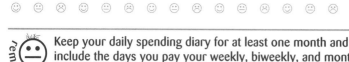

 Keep your daily spending diary for at least one month and make sure you include the days you pay your weekly, biweekly, and monthly bills. At the end of the month, evaluate your spending habits. See the "Evaluating Where Your Money Goes" section for details.

Using Other Tools to Track Your Spending

Did you realize that your bank and credit card statements can help you track your spending? Rather than just checking to make sure that the amounts are correct, you can use these records to see how much money you spend in each category. You can create simple categories by using different colors of highlighter or placing codes next to each expense: food, transportation, utilities, household, and miscellaneous.

Using the information that you gather, you can evaluate where your money goes (see the "Evaluating Where Your Money Goes" section later in this chapter).

 The time you invest now to gather information and track your spending pays off in easier budgeting and decision-making later.

Evaluating Where Your Money Goes

With your spending diary and bank records/credit card statements in hand, you can track your spending. Keep in mind that knowing where your money goes can help you keep it from going!

Table 2-3 is for you to track your spending. Adding each category for your month-long spending diary, plus looking at bank and credit card records, figure your expenses in each category for the month and place in the "Monthly" category. To estimate how much that adds up to for the year, simply multiply by 12. Prepare to be shocked at how much you're spending in some categories!

Some expenses, such as insurance payment, membership dues, gifts, and tuition, may occur only once or twice per year, so they may not appear in your daily spending diary. If any of these types of expenses listed in Table 2-3 apply to you, do a little research by looking through old bank statements or receipts and add the yearly amount to the table.

 In order to get a jump-start on Chapter 3, in which you create your first budget, you may want to fill out the lower portion of Table 2-3. That area asks you to record any income that you may receive on a monthly or yearly basis. If all you want to do is track your spending, however, you can ignore that section.

Table 2-3 Where My Money Is Going

Expense	Monthly	Yearly
Housing		
Rent or mortgage	_____	_____
Homeowner's/condo association dues	_____	_____
Maintenance	_____	_____
Property taxes	_____	_____
Insurance	_____	_____
Furniture and appliances	_____	_____
Utilities		
Gas	_____	_____
Electricity	_____	_____
Water	_____	_____
Garbage	_____	_____
Sewer	_____	_____
Telephone	_____	_____
Food		
Groceries	_____	_____
Eating out	_____	_____
Snacks and beverages	_____	_____
Transportation		
Automobile lease/payment 1	_____	_____
Automobile lease/payment 2	_____	_____

Expense	Monthly	Yearly
Transportation		
Licensing	_____	_____
Insurance	_____	_____
Maintenance	_____	_____
Gasoline	_____	_____
Public transportation	_____	_____
Parking/tolls	_____	_____
Health		
Doctor(s)	_____	_____
Dentist(s)	_____	_____
Medications	_____	_____
Insurance	_____	_____
Education		
Tuition/school fees	_____	_____
Books and supplies	_____	_____
School activities	_____	_____
Personal		
Clothing	_____	_____
Haircuts	_____	_____
Cosmetics	_____	_____
Pets	_____	_____
Childcare	_____	_____
Child support	_____	_____
Allowances	_____	_____
Gifts	_____	_____
Donations	_____	_____

continued

Table 2-3 *(continued)*

Expense	Monthly	Yearly
Personal		
Membership dues	_____	_____
Magazine and newspapers	_____	_____
Laundry/dry cleaning	_____	_____
Other _____	_____	_____
Savings and Investment Contributions		
Contributions to savings accounts	_____	_____
Contributions to 401(k)	_____	_____
Contributions to IRA(s)	_____	_____
Contributions to stocks	_____	_____
Contributions to mutual funds	_____	_____
Contributions to bonds	_____	_____
Other _____	_____	_____
Credit and Loan Payments		
Credit card 1	_____	_____
Credit card 2	_____	_____
Credit card 3	_____	_____
Department store card	_____	_____
Gasoline card	_____	_____
Student loan	_____	_____
Other _____	_____	_____
TOTAL EXPENSES	_____	_____
Income		
Wages, total	_____	_____
Gratuities	_____	_____

Expense	Monthly	Yearly
Income		
Dividends and interest	_____	_____
Social security	_____	_____
Pension	_____	_____
Trust fund	_____	_____
Royalties	_____	_____
Child support/alimony paid to you	_____	_____
Gifts	_____	_____
TOTAL INCOME	_____	_____

 You can add, subtract, or rearrange items to create a worksheet that fits your particular situation.

Now you know how much you're spending in each category. Chapter 3 helps you create a budget based on what you *want* to spend in each category and adjust your spending habits accordingly, keeping careful track if you overspend or underspend in a category.

Part 1: Figuring Out Your Finances

☺ ☹ ☹ ☺ ☹ ☹ ☺ ☹ ☹ ☺ ☹ ☹ ☺ ☹ ☹ ☺ ☺ ☹ ☹ ☺

Chapter 3

Creating a Budget

In This Chapter

☺ Determining essential and nonessential spending

☺ Planning for emergency expenses

☺ Creating a basic budget

C hapters 1 and 2 help you gather and organize information about your current financial situation and track how and where you're currently spending money. (If you haven't read those chapters and you need to gather more information about your finances, flip to Chapters 1 and 2 before starting this one.) In this chapter, you use financial information you've gathered to create a budget.

Budgeting is based on the basic principal that you categorize your expenses into essential and nonessential, and then begin to eliminate the nonessential ones to free up money to help you reach your financial goals — from finally starting a savings account (to pay for emergency expenses that may crop up from time to time) to building the home of your dreams to retiring at whatever age you choose.

Determining Your Essential Expenses: What You Need

Essential expenses are those obligations that you must pay regularly: weekly, monthly, semiannually (twice per year), or annually. Your essential expenses can be broken into two types: fixed and variable:

❀ **Fixed essential expenses are the same month after month.**
They include your rent or mortgage payment, car payment, property taxes, student loan payment, insurance (home, car, life, medical, and so on), and some utilities (for example, your phone bill may be the same every month). If your income doesn't vary from paycheck to paycheck, your taxes may also be fixed expenses that are taken out of your paycheck.

- *Variable* **essential expenses are due every week or month, but the amounts vary from month to month.** Variable essential expenses include groceries, utilities (gas, electricity, water, phone bill, including long-distance charges), gasoline for your car, expenses for your children at school, clothing, haircuts, and so on.

Note that money you put into a savings account to prepare for retirement or to save for large expenses, such as furniture, appliances, a new car, or a down payment on a house can be either fixed or variable, depending on how you save. You can find more on this in the "Paying yourself first" section.

In order to budget for variable expenses, you have to *prorate* (average out) these expenses to get a monthly or weekly average. Do so by figuring your yearly cost first: Review your bills for the last year and add up each month's or each week's bills so that you have a total for the year. (Note that you may also want to assume next year's expenses will be a little higher than your total for last year, given that inflation tends to drive up the cost of goods each year.) You then divide the yearly amount by 12 (if you want to develop a monthly budget) or 52 (if you want to start a weekly budget).

Factoring in emergency expenses

Emergencies will happen, whether you plan for them or not. And emergency expenses are essential: If your refrigerator breaks down, your dog needs to go to the vet, or you need to pay the co-payment on an emergency prescription, you have to spend that money.

Taking taxes into account

Most people have their taxes deducted from their paychecks and don't need to deal with them separately until they file their tax returns, so they don't think of taxes as an expense. If, however, you have a job that doesn't deduct taxes from your paychecks or if you have income from investments or your own business, you need to pay quarterly taxes to the government in April, June, September, and January. Otherwise, you'll have a big tax bill at the end of the year, along with even bigger penalties for not paying as you go.

If you're getting refunds — especially large refunds (you get to define *large* for yourself) — you need to make adjustments so that the taxes you pay throughout the year better reflect what you owe. A refund is not "found money"; it is money that you lent to the government without earning interest on it. You wouldn't put your money in a 0-percent-interest savings account, so don't loan the government money at no interest. Ideally, you'll tweak the amount taken out so that you don't owe any money, but you also don't receive a refund.

Chapter 3: Creating a Budget

The only way to not let emergency expenses blow your budget is to save for them. The budget you create in the "Setting Up a Basic Budget" section later in this chapter reflects that emergencies do happen, so you need to set aside savings to pay for such contingencies.

One of the biggest money-eaters in the emergency category can be your automobile, especially if it isn't maintained properly and regularly. To get a handle on how much you need to budget for care car, go through your car expenses for the last year. Include repairs, regular service (whether done at a service station or by you), and tire purchases to be sure you get a good idea of how much you're spending — on average — on emergency car expenses. Also review your car's service manual to be certain that you're following the manufacturer's recommendations.

Keep in mind that, depending on the age of your car, your warranty may cover some expenses. If a shop wants to add chargeable parts or labor to those covered by the warranty, ask to see the part that needs to be replaced and ask why. And if the needed repairs are costly, you may want to get a second opinion from another mechanic.

Keep similar records on all your major appliances and furniture, so that you can not only see what emergency expenses you've paid in the past but also predict when you will need to have money for future replacements. If your TV is 15 years old, chances are it's not going to last much longer! Table 3-1 helps you track the information you need to plan replacement purchases.

When you have an idea of how much money you need to keep in a savings account to be able to pay cash for these items as you need them, you can put these amounts in your budget. To make sure you keep this money strictly for emergencies, consider setting up a household expenses fund at the bank, one that's separate from any other savings accounts.

Notice that emergencies — real or imagined — always get paid somehow. If an insurance payment came due and it was larger than you expected, for example, you scrimped on restaurant meals or entertainment so that you had enough money to pay that important bill before your insurance was canceled. Keep this in mind when you're looking for ways to cut your expenses. What else could you scrimp on if the situation weren't an emergency — like saving for a down payment on a new house? See Chapter 4 for more on reducing your expenses.

Table 3-1 Major Purchases/Replacement Needs

Item	Date Purchased	Warranty Length	Expected Life	Purchase Price	Replacement Cost	Expected Replacement Date
Answering machine						
Central air conditioner or window unit						
Clothes dryer						
Clothes washer						
Computer						
Dishwasher						
DVD player or VCR						
Furnace						
Garage door opener						
Lawn mower						
Microwave						
Printer						
Recliner(s)						
Refrigerator						
Roof						

☺ ☺ ☹ ☺ ☺ ☹ ☺ ☺ ☹ ☺ ☺ ☹ ☺ ☺ ☹ ☺ ☺ ☺ ☹ ☺

Item	Date Purchased	Warranty Length	Expected Life	Purchase Price	Replacement Cost	Expected Replacement Date
Sofa(s)						
Stereo						
Stove						
Sump pump						
Television						
Vacuum cleaner						
Water heater						

Paying yourself first

Paying yourself first is one of the best money-management decisions you can make. Simply put, paying yourself first means that you set up a budget so that you put money into a savings program to meet your short-term, mid-term, and long-term goals *before* you pay anything else — including your rent or mortgage. If you're living from paycheck to paycheck, you may think that you can't do this, but as you look at nonessential expenses in the following section and set up your budget in the "Setting Up a Basic Budget" section, you may find the money to do this.

Money in your savings account is there to help you reach your financial goals, so you don't want to spend it whenever the department store at the mall has a great sale. On the other hand, if you find in a given month that you haven't stuck to your budget and you have to decide between paying your mortgage or putting money into savings, pay the mortgage! You don't want to lose your house while you're socking money into savings.

When you build up a savings account (and you will!), you'll lower your stress, feel much more stability, enjoy greater financial security, and feel better all around. Those feelings are worth the effort of creating and maintaining a budget.

Determining Your Nonessential Expenses: What You Want

After you pay your essential expenses, from the money that's left over, you pay your *nonessential* (also called *discretionary*) *expenses*, including the following:

- ❀ Certain nonessential utilities, such as cable, satellite, Internet access, and a cell phone
- ❀ Books, magazines, and newspaper subscriptions
- ❀ Restaurant meals; gourmet food from the grocery store or other shop
- ❀ Movies and concerts
- ❀ Some types of clothing, shoes, bags
- ❀ Gifts
- ❀ Vacations
- ❀ Hobbies

The key to being able to save money is determining which expenses you think of as essential (say, clothing or your car payment), really should be considered nonessential (if your wardrobe is stuffed or you're driving an expensive car that you could trade in for a much more economical one). Chapter 4 can help you reduce your expenses.

 The whole point of a budget is to have a plan for your money before you spend it. Without a budget, you can leave the house with $200 in cash, come back five hours later, and be able to account for only half that amount. With a budget, you'll be able to make firm spending decisions based on criteria that you have already set for yourself.

Setting Up a Basic Budget

This section shows you how to set up a budget that reflects the reality of your current financial life. Using Table 3-2, insert the information you've gathered about your expenses (see Chapter 2) and also insert information about your income.

1   Insert the values for what you paid in each category last month in the Last Month Actual column.

(If the expense was variable and you've been able to figure a monthly average, insert that amount.) Do this for every category that applies to you, and then total the list, seeing whether you have enough income to pay for your current expenses. (And if you're putting a lot of expenses on a credit card and not paying it off, you may actually be spending more than you're making.)

2   Note the categories in Table 3-2 for which you don't have an expense listed for the Last Month Actual column, but in which you'd like to start spending.

For example, any of the categories in Savings and Investments, insurance (if you're currently uninsured or underinsured), charitable contributions, or vacations may be areas you want to save or spend toward your goals.

3   Place the amounts in these new categories under the This Month Budget column.

4   Now comes the hard part: Figure out which expenses you can cut in order to pay for these additional savings or new expenses.

Determine what expenses you're going to cut or by how much you're going to reduce certain categories (Chapter 4 helps you do that), and put those amounts in the This Month Budget column.

Also fill in the rest of the categories in the This Month Budget column — the ones that aren't going to change anytime soon, like your mortgage payment.

5   And now an even harder part: Stick to your budget.

Over the next month, put the amount that you actually spend in each category in the This Month Actual column. Use the Over/Under column to compare the amount you meant to spend in each category to the amount you did spend. (Subtract This Month Actual from This Much Budget in each category.) If you're sticking to your budget perfectly, these Over/Under columns will all say 0!

Note that not all of the categories in Table 3-2 apply to you. Choose categories that reflect *your* situation (your current situation and the financial situation you want to be in) and cross through all the rest.

 Often, your mortgage, property taxes, waste removal fees, and insurance are lumped together in one payment. Don't "charge" yourself twice if you pay these expenses as part of your mortgage payments. Just list them under "Mortgage or rent."

Table 3-2 My Monthly Budget

Expense	Last Month Actual	This Month Budget	This Month Actual	Over/ Under
Housing and Utilities				
Mortgage or rent	$_____	_____	_____	_____
Homeowner's or condo assn. fees	$_____	_____	_____	_____
Home maintenance	$_____	_____	_____	_____
Electricity	$_____	_____	_____	_____
Gas	$_____	_____	_____	_____
Water	$_____	_____	_____	_____
Garbage removal	$_____	_____	_____	_____
Sewer fees	$_____	_____	_____	_____
Telephone	$_____	_____	_____	_____
Subtotal, Housing and Utilities	$_____	_____	_____	_____

☺ ☺ ☹ ☺ ☺ ☹ ☺ ☺ ☹ ☺ ☺ ☹ ☺ ☺ ☹ ☺ ☺ ☺ ☹ ☺

Expense	Last Month Actual	This Month Budget	This Month Actual	Over/ Under
Food				
Groceries	$_____	_____	_____	_____
Restaurant meals	$_____	_____	_____	_____
Subtotal, Food	$_____	_____	_____	_____
Clothing and Shoes				
Adult 1	$_____	_____	_____	_____
Adult 2	$_____	_____	_____	_____
Child 1	$_____	_____	_____	_____
Child 2	$_____	_____	_____	_____
Subtotal, Clothing and Shoes	$_____	_____	_____	_____
Child Care	$_____	_____	_____	_____
Insurance				
Auto	$_____	_____	_____	_____
Health	$_____	_____	_____	_____
Homeowner's/ renter's	$_____	_____	_____	_____
Life	$_____	_____	_____	_____
Other	$_____	_____	_____	_____
Subtotal, Insurance	$_____	_____	_____	_____
Healthcare				
Dentist	$_____	_____	_____	_____
Doctor	$_____	_____	_____	_____
Optometrist	$_____	_____	_____	_____
Other practitioner	$_____	_____	_____	_____
Eyeglasses, contacts	$_____	_____	_____	_____
Prescriptions	$_____	_____	_____	_____
Other	$_____	_____	_____	_____
Subtotal, Healthcare	$_____	_____	_____	_____

continued

27

Table 3-2 My Monthly Budget (continued)

Expense	Last Month Actual	This Month Budget	This Month Actual	Over/ Under
Auto				
Payment 1	$_____	_____	_____	_____
Payment 2	$_____	_____	_____	_____
Gasoline 1	$_____	_____	_____	_____
Gasoline 2	$_____	_____	_____	_____
Maintenance 1	$_____	_____	_____	_____
Maintenance 2	$_____	_____	_____	_____
Tolls	$_____	_____	_____	_____
Taxis and other public transportation	$_____	_____	_____	_____
Subtotal, Auto	$_____	_____	_____	_____
Personal				
Charitable contributions	$_____	_____	_____	_____
Cosmetics	$_____	_____	_____	_____
Entertainment	$_____	_____	_____	_____
Haircuts	$_____	_____	_____	_____
Magazines, newspapers	$_____	_____	_____	_____
Organization dues	$_____	_____	_____	_____
Vacations	$_____	_____	_____	_____
Other	$_____	_____	_____	_____
Subtotal, Personal	$_____	_____	_____	_____
Savings and Investments				
Savings/money market account	$_____	_____	_____	_____
Education fund	$_____	_____	_____	_____
Mutual fund	$_____	_____	_____	_____
New car fund	$_____	_____	_____	_____

Chapter 3: Creating a Budget

☺ ☺ ☹ ☺ ☺ ☹ ☺ ☺ ☹ ☺ ☺ ☹ ☺ ☺ ☹ ☺ ☺ ☹ ☺

Expense	Last Month Actual	This Month Budget	This Month Actual	Over/ Under
Savings and Investments				
New home fund	$_____	_____	_____	_____
Retirement fund	$_____	_____	_____	_____
Emergency savings account	$_____	_____	_____	_____
Other	$_____	_____	_____	_____
Subtotal, Savings and Investments	$_____	_____	_____	_____
Taxes				
Federal income tax	$_____	_____	_____	_____
State income tax	$_____	_____	_____	_____
Local income tax	$_____	_____	_____	_____
Social Security tax	$_____	_____	_____	_____
Self-employment tax	$_____	_____	_____	_____
Property tax	$_____	_____	_____	_____
Subtotal, Taxes	$_____	_____	_____	_____
TOTAL EXPENSES	$_____	_____	_____	_____
Income				
Gross wages 1	$_____	_____	_____	_____
Gross wages 2	$_____	_____	_____	_____
Interest income	$_____	_____	_____	_____
Alimony/Child support paid to you	$_____	_____	_____	_____
Other	$_____	_____	_____	_____
TOTAL INCOME	$_____	_____	_____	_____
Difference between income and expenses (put shortages in parentheses)	$_____	_____		_____

29

Budgeting software

Computers can do many things for you. Luckily, keeping track of your budget is one of them! Programs like Quicken, Budget, and Microsoft Money are inexpensive yet flexible, and most create a budget for you according to your specifications.

Depending on the software package you buy, you can compare your planned spending with actual spending in any category, highlight when expenses are due, monitor your loan payments, manage your investments, and create reports and graphs to show how you're progressing toward your goals.

On the other hand, paper and pencil work just fine, and they do save you the cost of buying software. Whatever you decide, don't put off budgeting because you don't have a computer or haven't bought the software. Low-tech is good, too.

Make sure to account for all your expenses, putting them in any category that makes your budget work for you. For example, you may want to put your homeowner's or renter's insurance under "Housing and Utilities" rather than under "Insurance." Also, as you recognize new items, add them to your budget.

Being Realistic

Keep in mind that if your budget doesn't reflect reality and you can't live within the boundaries you set, it's useless. How does a budget become and remain realistic? When the figures you enter in your budget reflect reality and not wishful thinking, when you're willing to spend time updating your budget regularly, and when you recognize that changes need to be made (and then make them!).

Part 2

We're Moving On Up: Putting Your Budget to Work

Believe it or not, running your finances within the friendly confines of a budget can be liberating. After you're in the habit of knowing where it has been going and decide where you want it to start going, you can make wise money decisions every day without the stress of wondering how you're going to pay for them.

In this part, you find out how to stick to your budget. You also find ways to reduce your expenses without lowering your quality of life, so that you can do the most with your money. Most importantly, I help you reduce your debt and start saving for retirement, a new home, or whatever your goals may be.

Chapter 4

Knowing When to Hold 'Em: Sticking to Your Budget

In This Chapter

☺ Understanding the role of self-discipline

☺ Recognizing and avoiding hidden expenses

☺ Finding helpful resources

Realizing that you need a budget, gathering your information, and putting that information into a usable form are giant strides toward securing your financial future. This chapter shows you how to build on the foundation that you established by creating a budget.

Good Discipline Equals Good Budgeting

You have many good habits that took time to cultivate. You may not even recognize that you have these habits, because after you've developed a good habit, you don't really think about it (unless you start to lose it). Give yourself credit for developing habits such as the following:

❀ I brush my teeth every day.

❀ I change the oil in my car regularly.

❀ I get to work on time.

In the interest of appreciating that you can pick up good budgeting habits, too, use the following list to check off any that you've already developed:

❀ I pay my bills on time.

❀ I balance my checkbook.

❀ I compare prices when I shop.

None of these habits by itself makes your life either wonderful or awful. But adding good habits on top of good habits improves your life immensely.

You can't just fling your old bad habits out the window. To become an effective budgeter, you must coax yourself into developing good habits. Check off the following activities that you can accomplish:

✼ Recognize how budgeting benefits me

✼ Notice changes in my spending habits and decide whether the changes are good or bad

✼ Revise my budget when my circumstances change

✼ Write down changes that I want to make instead of keeping them in my head

Failing to use and revise your budget has many drawbacks:

✼ You waste the time that you already spent collecting data.

✼ You miss out on the many benefits that budgeting brings to your financial life, such as the ability to use decisions you've made instead of reacting to situations.

✼ Your stress level rises.

Making Over Your Lifestyle

Giving your lifestyle a makeover is *not* the same as lowering your standard of living or depriving yourself. In fact, it can be quite the opposite. The emphasis here is on the *style* part of your lifestyle. The following sections can help you reduce your expenses and at the same time improve the *style* in your life.

Using coupons rather than paying full price

The art of saving money by using coupons has become a consumer industry in itself. Whether you've never used coupons or you use them regularly and want to get more from your efforts, the tips in this section can help you meet your goals.

Couponing is a skill that can pay off financially. Here's how:

1 Find coupon sources.

Check the Internet, newspapers (especially the Sunday paper), the telephone book, the packaging of items you've already bought, the back of your supermarket receipts, and coupon trade boxes inside stores, to name a few sources. You can also ask friends and family to save particular coupons that are important to you, for example, diaper coupons.

2   Organize your coupons.

Get a 3 x 5 file box with dividers for each category (say, "Frozen foods" or "Sauces and Spreads") or a specially made coupon organizer and file your coupons each time you cut them out. Coupon experts often recommend filing them by earliest expiration date first within each category, so that you don't overlook soon-to-expire coupons.

3   Use your coupons when you shop.

Make sure you always have your coupons with you, even if you're just making a quick trip into a store.

 You can get more than face value for your coupons by shopping at stores that double coupons, or give you twice what the coupon is worth.

 Don't buy something just because you have a coupon for it, especially if it's too expensive to begin with. If you won't use the product for a while, you have to store it; if it's something you don't like, you'll never use it.

Recognizing and avoiding hidden expenses

Hidden expenses are those sneaky money-eaters that lurk everywhere. Knowing what and where they hide and how much they cost helps you cut them by avoiding the items to which they are attached.

Bank, ATM, and credit card fees

Hidden costs at banks, at ATMs, and on credit cards can quickly transfer your money from your pocket to an institution's profit statement. Be careful of

❋   Annual fees

❋   Below-minimum-use and below-minimum-balance fees

❋   High interest rates

❋   Late-payment penalties

❋   Per-use fees

 Read all change-of-terms inserts that you receive from banks, credit unions, credit card companies, and the like. The information that they contain may be a call to change how and where you do business.

35

Not knowing what fees you're liable for with your money-handling institutions is the same as using a credit card without knowing what rate of interest you're paying. If you don't carry a balance on your credit card, the interest rate is irrelevant. If you don't incur fees from your bank and so on, you don't care what that fee is, either. But you need to know what and how much they are so that you know how to avoid them.

Gratuities, delivery charges, and taxes

The more convenience services you use, the more you'll pay in *gratuities* (tips) and delivery charges. Having meals or groceries delivered is convenient and may save you time, but in addition to paying for what you eat, you pay for delivery costs and a tip for the delivery person — neither of which you can have for dessert.

Catalog shopping can save a lot of time, too, along with parking and car-use costs. An add-on cost, however, may be shipping charges (often unrecoverable if you return the item). And if you do return the item, you may need to pay insurance costs as well to protect against the item getting lost or damaged in transit. Plus, when you buy something in a store, you can inspect it before you take it home. And you can watch for sales.

 This doesn't mean that you should always shop in stores; it just means that you need to know and compare the costs of various ways of taking care of your needs. If you use the time you save to earn more income, for example, the convenience may be worth the cost.

As for taxes, not all items are taxed at the same rate. Grocery food, for example, is not taxed in some states and is taxed at a lower rate than other items in other states. Yet prepared food is often taxed, so in addition to paying for the preparation of food in a restaurant, you're also paying more in taxes than you would if you bought groceries and cooked at home.

State legislatures have designated some items as *luxury items.* Liquor is a common example. Read your receipts carefully. Some cash registers print the added taxes next to each item purchased so that you can readily see how much you're paying for items. You may decide to reduce or eliminate these heavily taxed items from your lifestyle.

 Choosing one item over another may not save you a ton of money, but making decisions about saving over and over can help you reach your financial goals.

Remembering that you don't have to spend a lot to have fun

When you first determined to get your financial house in order, you probably thought that entertainment and vacations would go by the wayside in order for you to reach your financial goals. Not true!

☺ ☺ ☹ ☺ ☺ ☹ ☺ ☺ ☹ ☺ ☺ ☹ ☺ ☺ ☹ ☺ ☺ ☺ ☹ ☺

Look for your opportunities to reduce your expenses without reducing your quality of life. Instead of always looking to your wallet to pay for entertainment, use the creative skills that you've been developing. Knowledgeable, reliable people are in demand everywhere.

✸ **Volunteer for the arts.** If theater, opera, live music, and so on are your passion, you can enjoy them without blowing your budget or dipping into savings. Many events use volunteer ushers. If you usher, you attend for free. (The downside is that you may have to see the same play ten times — and you can't walk out on a stinker.) Do you like music? Offer to be a music page turner for rehearsal sessions. In the long run, however, you'll have a good time for only the price of transportation or parking.

If you can't devote the time to be a regular usher at the theater, offer a skill or time in trade for attending a dress rehearsal.

✸ **Work at sporting events.** If you like sports, find out what personnel are needed to put on an event. Could you hold the measuring chains at football games? Does a track meet need a timer?

✸ **Go back to school.** Do you live near a school that needs monitors to take students to see matinees or go to museums? Volunteer for the job.

✸ **Take a last-minute trip.** Some travel agencies sell off cruises and other deals at very good prices to people who can fill vacancies at the last minute. You can buy into these deals at 50 percent or more off the listed price.

Sometimes, you have to become a member of a travel club in order to be notified of an opening. Before joining, make sure you will use or save enough to make the membership fees worthwhile.

Living on less

If you went to the store to buy one size and brand of bread and could pay $2.00 or $2.50 for it, which would you choose? This sounds like a simple question, yet people make the wrong decision every day.

Here are some ways to live on less without sacrificing quality of life:

✸ **Shop at discount stores instead of convenience stores** and buy the same items for less. Head to the library for a local or area-wide directory of discount and outlet stores.

✸ **Take your lunch instead of buying it;** you'll eat a healthier lunch and save money, too.

✸ **Negotiate with your employer to work at home.** By doing so, you can save restaurant, travel, car wear and tear, and clothing expenses.

 Decide beforehand who will pay for the equipment, telephone lines, and other expenses. If those expenses are your responsibility, you may be spending instead of saving money.

❀ **Buy a used car the next time you're ready for one.** A used car is "new" to you. You not only pay less, but the insurance costs are less than on a new car, depreciation is slower, and you don't have to dread that first ding in the door.

❀ **Understand your real goal before you make a purchase.** If you want to lose weight, for example, you can do so for free by walking in the park or by taking advantage of the company gym. Either one is cheaper than signing a contract at a health club.

Reining In Your Impulse Spending

If, every time you return from the store, you find that you have more items than you intended to purchase, you're not entirely at fault. Store managers have studied consumers for years. Stores purposely develop floor plans that tempt you to buy things you didn't know you wanted and expose you to as many buying opportunities as possible.

 Don't confuse good buys with impulse purchases. If you find a closeout on something your family uses and you can use it all before it spoils, that's a good buying decision, unless it means that you can't pay another bill and will have to pay a penalty fee on that bill.

Recognizing your triggers

Most impulse buys are the results of *triggers* — conditions that make you more prone to spending money. The following list of common triggers may seem familiar.

❀ **Celebration:** You or your friend/sibling/cousin/college roommate deserves a nice present to celebrate a birthday/anniversary/new job.

❀ **Competition:** You have to give the nicest gift, or at least one that's as nice as so-and-so's.

❀ **Depression:** You try to make yourself feel better by buying yourself a treat.

❀ **Desire to impress someone:** You think, "Wait until so-and-so sees this!"

❀ **Elation:** You think that nothing can go wrong when you feel so good, so you have a treat.

☺ ☺ ☹ ☺ ☺ ☹ ☺ ☺ ☹ ☺ ☺ ☹ ☺ ☺ ☹ ☺ ☺ ☺ ☹ ☺

❀ **Fatigue:** You've worked hard, so you feel that you deserve a treat.

❀ **Money in your pocket:** You have the cash to pay for it, so why not have a treat?

Ensuring that you meet your long-term financial goals is the best "treat" you can give yourself!

You probably know the kinds of items you're most likely to purchase on a whim. Walk around the house and write down those things that you've purchased impulsively so that you can see how much money you've wasted by not making thoughtful decisions. Write down every item that falls into your impulse-spending category. You don't need to go through every door or find every impulse purchase, but do use Table 4-1 to write down all the impulse buys that you find in plain sight.

Table 4-1 Tracking Your Impulse Spending

Item	Trigger for Purchasing the Item	Approximate Cost	Worthwhile? (+)	Not Worthwhile? (*)

39

For example, are clothes your weakness? How many items did you buy that were on sale but that don't really work well with the rest of your wardrobe? Do you find it impossible to pass by a gourmet food shop? Many expensive items in trendy shops are available for much less in superstores. What about books? Sure, you want to buy some books to keep, but are there any you could get at your local library, instead?

If you do this exercise with your family, reassure everyone before you start that its only purpose is to gather information. If you use the information to find fault with your or others' purchases, you'll defeat the purpose and discourage helpful suggestions.

After you've compiled your list of impulse purchases, follow these steps:

1 **Write an estimated cost next to each item.**

2 **Put a plus sign (+) next to anything you think you've used as much as you should have for the price.**

   For example, you may have used your snow blower every time it snowed, but that may mean that each five-minute snow-removal job has cost you $87 — no + there. And don't forget the cost to insure that expensive piece of equipment.

3 **Put an asterisk (*) next to each item for which you could have purchased a reasonable substitute at a lower cost.**

   Sometimes, a small investment of time can result in paying a much lower price.

4 **Next to the asterisk, write the price you think that you could have paid for a reasonable substitute.**

   Don't put garage-sale or second-hand-sale prices here — you have no guarantee that you would have found a comparable substitute.

Don't ignore small impulse purchases. Although you may not have included low-costs items in this list, you may purchase them more often than big-ticket items, so they add up quickly.

Focusing on your goals

If in Chapter 1, you made a list of your short-term, mid-term, and long-term goals, go back to that list now. You may have gathered other information since writing those goals, so you may want to revise the list before you work on eliminating impulse spending. Whether or not you revise the list, look at your goals now.

Starting at the top of your list, apply the "overspent" amount from Table 4-1 to pay for your goals, whether your goals are to pay off your debts, save more, start investing, or purchase something that you really need or want. You may need to take more than one overspent amount to make up one goal amount. Don't bother to prioritize your goals here; you just want to know how many goals you could have checked off your list if you hadn't made impulse purchases. For example, not buying that snow blower may have paid for two car payments.

Stopping yourself from making a purchase

After you recognize what triggers make you indulge in impulse spending and what the payoff can be when you make informed purchases based on your financial goals, you can control your impulse purchase. Do so by making conscious decisions before the temptation to buy reaches out to grab you.

Stopping your impulse spending doesn't mean that you never get to treat yourself. If the supermarket is your downfall, for example, give yourself a set amount to spend any way you like. After a few trips to the store during which you can't decide which one treat you want, you may find that you don't want any of them all that much!

Hanging onto your found money

The fastest way to undo all your hard work is to think of your money as a tradeoff between spending on one item and spending on another. In other words, just because you save in one area, don't immediately think of that money as being available to spend in another area.

If you reduce your expenses, you may feel rich because you at last have cash in your pocket. But instead of spending your new-found wealth, that money should go first toward debt reduction (which Chapter 5 discusses in depth). After you're out of debt, don't look for places to spend the newly released money; you've already promised that money to your savings plan (see Chapter 6).

Does paying off debts and then putting money toward savings mean that you don't get to enjoy the fruits of your labor? Of course not. You get to enjoy seeing your debts disappear, watching your savings grow, and achieving all the financial goals you've ever had.

While you're paying off debts and starting a savings program with your found money, don't even think about the credit available on your credit cards. Using that credit means more debt, which is exactly what you don't want.

If your impulse triggers go off in a type of store that sells big-ticket items, again give yourself a treat budget that you save for. If you don't have enough money to buy what you want today, you can save up your treat allowance until you have enough money in that "account." But you don't get to buy now and pay with your future allowance.

Always use a shopping list. Just as the lines on the highway keep you driving in the lane, a shopping list can keep you from giving in to temptation. Even if you decide to purchase something that's not on your list, you'll at least have considered and weighed the purchase.

Dealing with Emergency Expenses

Unexpected expenses can severely disrupt your financial status. The three situations that usually get people in financial trouble are healthcare emergencies, expensive appliances that wear out, and vehicle repair and replacement.

Those expenses are the reason you have an emergency expense fund. (If you don't, flip to Chapter 3 and find out about budgeting for emergencies.) If your savings account isn't large enough when you do have an emergency, however, you can take short-term actions to avoid ending up in a spiral of debt:

❀ Hold a garage sale. You may be able to clean out your house and make a few hundred dollars at the same time. Keep in mind, though, that a good garage sale takes at least two or three full days of preparation.

❀ See whether you can work overtime or get a part-time temporary job to pay for the expense. Although you'll be busy and tired, you may just be able to pay for your emergency without going into debt.

❀ Pawn some possessions. Pawning is really a secured loan — you get cash in exchange for an item of value. If you pay back the loan (with interest, of course) by the deadline, you can retrieve your item.

❀ If you have a medical emergency, ask your healthcare provider about available services that would offset expenses for you, such as free or low-cost housing and meals while your loved one is in the hospital.

❀ If your problem is with your car and you have a good relationship with a garage, try to negotiate a time-payment plan at low or no interest (rather than the higher rate that you would pay on a credit card).

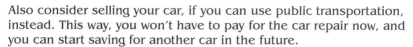
Also consider selling your car, if you can use public transportation, instead. This way, you won't have to pay for the car repair now, and you can start saving for another car in the future.

❋ If your income is low, ask your local government or social services agency if low- or no-interest loans are available for these types of emergencies. Religious organizations may also have such funds.

❋ Ask your credit card companies and other creditors to let you skip a payment without penalty. They'll still add in an interest charge, which raises your total debt, but this tactic frees up immediate money so that you can take care of the emergency.

❋ If you belong to a social or service organization, find out whether it has a formal or informal system for helping members.

Paying for an emergency by credit card may get you in debt at a high interest rate. If you must use a credit card, be sure to choose the one with the lowest interest rate. Now may be the time to take advantage of a low-introductory-rate card that has been offered to you — but do so only if you can pay off the balance before the introductory rate expires, or if the regular rate is reasonable.

Rounding Up Your Support Team

All kinds of people and organizations are available to help you meet your goals and stick to your budget.

Spouse/significant other

Often, one partner is a better money manager than the other. That partner may be better at resisting temptation, computing amounts, breaking down long-term goals into short-term and mid-term ones, setting priorities, budget balancing, and so on. Or one partner may be better at some activities, while the other handles the remaining tasks.

The secret to a good partnership is agreeing to goals and how you're going to reach those goals (see Chapter 1). You may have to compromise on individual goals in order to reach your goals as a family. Then each partner does the best job possible for his or her responsibilities and with his or her skills. As time goes on and changes need to be made, use the same negotiating and compromise that brought you as far as you are to help you set up a new system.

Children

You certainly want to help children develop money-management skills. Keeping children involved in the budgeting process helps them understand the financial lessons that they need to know at each stage in their lives.

No child is too young to participate in the family budget. If your children are not part of your budgeting board of directors, everyone gets cheated. They not only miss out on important lessons, but their feelings and wishes aren't reflected in two strategic parts of family life: budgeting and buying decisions. However, the younger a child is, the shorter-term the goal must be to fit with a young child's short attention span and lack of patience.

Family and friends

Your parents have lived longer and have survived more financial challenges than you have, so they may be able to give you financial advice that makes sense. However, if they expect you to take whatever advice they give — and they will continue to give advice throughout the rest of their lives without your asking — you may want to steer clear.

Friends and other family members can be most helpful in not tempting you to spend money that's not in your budget. Explain your goals and plans to your family and friends and ask for specific support, such as recognizing a trigger (see the "Recognizing your triggers" section) and stopping you from making an impulse buy. You can also talk to them about cutting back on gift-giving, eating out, birthday parties, or whatever other expensive habits you may have developed with friends and family that you now want to cut back.

Professional and free services

Professional sources can help you gather information, set goals, establish priorities, and stay on your financial path. You can use these sources right now, use them as needed, or even discard them from your financial life after their purpose has been served.

Accountants do much more than fill out tax returns. They can help you set goals, remind you of factors that you have forgotten or ignored, start you on a good financial plan no matter what your age or income, help you revise your plans and goals as you get older, and — the part you'll probably enjoy the most — help you reduce the taxes you pay. Depending on the accountant, you may also be able to get information about estate planning, insurance practices, housing, healthcare, and scholarships.

☺ ☺ ☹ ☺ ☺ ☹ ☺ ☺ ☹ ☺ ☺ ☹ ☺ ☺ ☹ ☺ ☺ ☺ ☹ ☺

Your employer, union, or trade organization may have an *EAP (Employee Assistance Program)*. While the services that an EAP offers vary from provider to provider, some EAPs offer budgeting, savings, tax, and estate-planning services, either individually or in groups. Whatever the topic, if you need information about it and don't pay for it, you've eliminated that budget expense while still finding the information you need.

Churches, temples, community groups, libraries, schools, alumni groups, financial institutions, credit bureaus, and associations (such as Masons, Eastern Star, and Rotary) may offer budgeting and savings programs, either for free or at a low cost. Look in local newspapers and newsletters for ads announcing such programs. Your local library or social service agency may also keep track of such listings.

If at First You Don't Succeed

The Greek philosopher Aristotle said, "We are what we repeatedly do. Excellence is not an act, but a habit." You've already taken the time and trouble to gather information, set goals, develop new techniques, and set a budget, so now's the time to turn your newfound skills into habits.

Popular knowledge says that cultivating a new habit takes 21 days, which means that by doing something every day, you can change your life in three short weeks. Some financial habits are cultivated daily — packing lunches versus eating out, taking the bus versus a taxi, watching a video instead of going to a movie, listening to the radio versus buying a new CD — which means that you can quickly develop good habits. Other financial matters — furniture and appliance shopping and choosing investment instruments — aren't tasks you do every day, so developing new habits may take a little longer.

Sometimes, instead of giving yourself credit for what you have accomplished, you may worry about what you still lack. Don't fall into this pit of disappointment. As you review your budget, take time to savor how far you've come, and then choose which habit you want to tackle next and concentrate on it.

Chapter 5

Knowing When to Fold 'Em: Tackling Your Debt

In order for you to reach your financial goals (see Chapter 1), you have to get yourself out of debt. Paying 12, 15, or 18 percent interest on credit cards or car loans doesn't make sense if you're also socking money away for retirement at 8 percent. So, except for putting away a little money in savings for emergencies (see Chapter 4), first pay off all your debt, and then begin saving for a new house, kids' college education, a new car, and/or retirement.

Figuring Out How Much You Owe

To find out how much you owe, the first step is to take a personal debt survey. This survey is a little easier than a budget survey because you need only your latest statement from each debt. Gather the following documents:

❋ Coupon book for your mortgage payments

❋ Coupon book(s) for your automobile payments

❋ Credit card statements

❋ Department store card statements

❋ Loan statements (If you haven't started paying back a loan yet or if your statements show only the monthly amount due, call the lender and ask for the total amount due.)

❋ Paperwork for private loans from relatives and friends (Keep good records so that no dispute occurs.)

Using Table 5-2, create a table that looks like Table 5-1:

Table 5-1 Sample Debt Register

Account	Total Amount Due	Monthly Payment	Total Interest Paid Last Year	Interest Rate
VISA	$4,568	$115	$639	12.9%
MasterCard	$2,372	$86	$481	15.9%
Home Repairs, Inc.	$1,423	$67	$314	18.5%
Car payment	$15,268	$236	$1,162	7.1%
Mortgage	$117,469	$916	$8,437	6.7%

Table 5-2 My Debt Register

Account	Total Amount Due	Monthly Payment	Total Interest Paid Last Year	Interest Rate

 To see how much your debt is costing you, call each lender and ask how much you paid in interest last year. Record those amounts in your debt register. Remember that you received no benefit from all that money you paid in interest.

Paying Off Your Credit Cards and Charge Accounts

Getting the balance on your credit cards down to $0 feels good. Because it seems to be a giant step toward the goal of having no *consumer debt* (which is defined as all money you owe *except* your mortgage), you may be tempted to pay off your lowest-balance credit card or charge account first. However, that is *not* the way to speed up the reduction of your debt.

Instead, the best payoff system is three-part:

1   Move balances from high-interest accounts to low-interest accounts, if you can.

2   Pay the minimum due on your low-interest accounts and pay as much as you can on your high-interest accounts until they're paid off.

3   After your high-interest accounts are paid off, pay as much as possible on your low-interest accounts until they're paid off.

By paying off your high-interest-rate cards first, you save the most money.

Tables 5-3 and 5-4 offer a comparison of how the interest rate affects your ability to pay off your debt. This example uses an interest rate that's computed monthly: Keep in mind that credit card companies and charge accounts often compute interest *daily*, which means that the interest due will usually be even higher.

Table 5-3 Your Debt Cost at 14.9 Percent Annual Interest

Month	Balance	Yearly Interest Rate ÷ 12	Interest Debt This Month	New Balance	Payment
1	$5,000.00	1.2416666%	$62.08	$5,062.08	$150.00
2	$4,912.08	1.2416666%	$60.99	$4,973.07	$150.00
3	$4,823.07	1.2416666%	$59.89	$4,882.96	$150.00
4	$4,732.96	1.2416666%	$58.77	$4,791.73	$150.00
5	$4,641.73	1.2416666%	$57.63	$4,699.36	$150.00
6	$4,549.36	1.2416666%	$56.49	$4,605.85	$150.00

Total interest paid in six months: $355.85

Total of payments for six months: $900.00

Percent of payoff that is interest: 39.5%

Stop using your credit cards

In order to pay off your credit cards, you need to not only work hard at paying off the balance but also stop adding to the debt. That means you have to stop using your credit cards. If you have to pay with cash, checks, or debit cards — all of which are limited to the funds you have now — you'll spend less. Take your credit cards out of your wallet and put them into storage. When you're out of debt, you can think about using them again.

As you develop your budgeting skills and have paid off all your consumer debt, use your credit cards again. Because your new way of handling credit cards will look good on your credit report, you'll be able to get lower-interest cards, lower-rate loans, and a lower-rate mortgage. Your good financial reputation will give you leverage to negotiate other financial deals. Don't start using one or two cards (that's all you need — destroy the rest), until you can resist overspending and unplanned spending.

Table 5-4 Your Debt Cost at 6.9 Percent Annual Interest

Month	Balance	Yearly Interest Rate ÷ 12	Interest Debt This Month	New Balance	Payment
1	$5,000.00	0.575%	$28.75	$5,028.75	$150.00
2	$4,878.75	0.575%	$28.05	$4,906.81	$150.00
3	$4,756.80	0.575%	$27.35	$4,784.15	$150.00
4	$4,634.15	0.575%	$26.65	$4,660.80	$150.00
5	$4,510.80	0.575%	$25.94	$4,536.74	$150.00
6	$4,386.74	0.575%	$25.23	$4,411.96	$150.00

Total interest paid in six months: $161.97

Total of payments for six months: $900.00

Percent of payoff that is interest: 18%

Table 5-4 shows that in just six months, you save $193.88 in interest charges by paying a 8 percent lower annual interest rate. From this example, you can see how first paying off your higher-rate cards saves you money, gets you out of debt faster, and helps you pay less interest.

An old adage says that if you owe enough money, your creditors become your partners. Call your credit card companies or the holders of your loans to ask for help in rescheduling your payments. Many companies help finance credit counseling services to help their customers (and themselves) by keeping you from filing bankruptcy. You can also contact your local Better Business Bureau for a list of its credit counselor members. These services charge a nominal fee that is often shared by your creditors. You can also look in the Yellow Pages under "Credit Counselors."

You can also get help from the nonprofit National Foundation for Consumer Credit Counseling. For help in English, call 800-388-2227; for help in Spanish, call 800-682-9832. You can also contact the foundation on the Internet at www.nfcc.org to get information or to find a service near you.

Do not use credit repair services that you see advertised on telephone poles and subway walls. They can't do anything that you can't either do yourself or use a legitimate credit-counseling service to do for you. On top of that, these fly-by-night firms charge hefty fees for their "service" — money that you could have used to pay down your debt. Legitimate counselors do not promise "credit repair," because the only way to earn a good credit rating is to pay your bills on time.

Many banks charge an annual fee on their credit cards if you pay off your monthly invoices so that you don't pay any interest. After yours is paid off, shop for a credit card that charges no annual fee, regardless of whether you carry a balance or pay it off.

As with other credit cards, you can use department store credit cards in a good way or a bad way. First, be aware that these cards tend to charge high interest rates. That doesn't mean that you shouldn't use them at all; just use them wisely and pay the balance (not just the minimum due) each month. Also be aware that holding such cards means that the stores will bombard you with mailings. You find out about sales, but you may be tempted to buy things that you don't need. You can, however, call the company and ask them to send you only your bills, not any advertisements.

If you're trying to rebuild your credit, department store cards can be a good way to do so. They're relatively easy to get — if your credit rating isn't good, you just get a low maximum. And these cards don't charge annual fees. The combination gives you a chance to charge carefully, pay religiously, and improve your credit history.

Department store card balances can sneak up on you. Along with high interest rates, these cards often have a low minimum payment due. But the longer you stretch out paying off the balance, the more interest you pay. Refer to Tables 5-3 and 5-4, which show that higher interest rates make a big difference in the amount you have to pay back.

Paying Back Your Loans

You handle loans like you handle credit card and charge account debt: You prioritize which loans to pay first, based on their rates. (The exception is mortgages, which you can read about in the "Mortgages" section later in this chapter.)

If you run into a rough patch financially, call your lenders and make deals for deferring payments *before* your payments are late. But be very careful when you negotiate. The interest rate on some loans rises automatically if you're late or you defer payment(s). Negotiate to keep your interest rate the same.

 When you've tallied six months or more of faithful payments, ask your creditors to lower your interest rates.

Student and educational loans

If you're sorry now that you took out those student loans, keep in mind that student loans are an investment in your future. Graduating from college is still a good investment, even after you pay off your loans. The following list shows the results of a 1999 Census Bureau release that calculated lifetime earnings according to educational level.

❀ High school: $1,200,000

❀ Bachelor's degree: $2,100,000

❀ Master's degree: $2,500,000

❀ Doctoral degree: $3,400,000

❀ Professional degree (medical, law): $4,400,000

And the gap is widening. So take a deep breath, roll up your sleeves, and put the loan payback into your budget.

If your only experience with timed payments is with car payments, you may think that your only repayment option is to pay equal amounts each month until your debt is paid. These are called *standard repayments*. The good news is that standard repayments are predictable. The bad news is that you're making payments when you're just out of school, trying to set up a household, buy a professional wardrobe, and start a professional life. So perhaps another repayment plan would suit your life better.

 Consider asking your lender for graduated payments. When you first get out of school and have high expenses and not-so-high income, making lower payments is easier. As you progress in your career, with presumably higher pay, your payments also increase.

Although this plan extends your payments, and you pay more in interest, it also arranges for you to match higher payments with higher income. As an added bonus, your good payment record enhances your overall credit rating. A good credit rating means that you'll be able to qualify for credit cards, mortgages, and other loans at lower interest rates than can people who have bad credit records.

Another possibility is a payment schedule based on your income. Student loans are guaranteed by the government agency Sallie Mae (Student Loan Marketing Association). This guarantee gives you the option of paying between 4 and 25 percent of your gross monthly income on your loan. Again, you'll pay more in interest over the length of the loan than you would with a standard repayment plan. But if you expect to start your career at a fairly low salary with the promise of salary growth, an income-based plan can help you keep your payments proportionate to your salary and your credit rating good.

The best news is that you don't have to choose a payment plan and stay with it. If your financial picture changes, you can probably negotiate a new plan. If your finances change drastically — for example, if you become ill or unemployed — you may even be able to defer some payments. Interest will continue accruing, but you should be able to negotiate waiving of late-payment penalties.

 Your best negotiating position is when you contact the lender, not when you get behind in your payments and the lender contacts you. Keeping track of your ability to pay and making adjustments to your payment plan before you have financial problems is the way to use your education debt to build a good credit report.

When paying off your consumer debt (that's all your debt except your mortgage), your student loan should probably be last on your list. Because the interest rate is low and interest is added only once a month, this is probably your lowest-cost loan.

Car loans

You probably need a car for transportation. Before you think about how much you can afford, you need to identify your needs (versus your desires) so that you can make good financial decisions and not bow to sales pressure. With a needs list in place, you can resist the sales pressure when you see all the goodies available.

 Before buying a car, look at the overall cost, as though you're paying cash for your car. Don't get sucked into the "little bit more" that it costs each month to have monogrammed floor mats (or whatever). Set a total price that you'll pay, regardless of the monthly payments. Because you have much higher financial goals than just being able to make your payments each month, the monthly payments that your salesperson will push are pretty irrelevant to you.

Shop around for loan rates before you go car shopping. Then you can focus your energies on one item at a time: first the loan, and then the car. When you secure the loan, make sure that there is no *prepayment penalty* (a penalty for paying off your loan early). Read your dealership or lender contract carefully to avoid additional fees and penalties. Also, make sure to tell the lender that all excess payments are to be applied to the principal portion of the loan so that your interest payments decrease even more with each payment. Mark this with a sticky-back note on your payment stub each month, too.

When you're deciding how to pay down your debts, evaluate the interest rate and compounding policy (the total cost of the loan). After you have this information, you can compare it to your other debts to prioritize loan repayments, paying off the debts with the highest interest rates first.

Mortgages

Your housing costs are part of the short-term, mid-term, and long-term goals you list in Chapter 1. But a budget is a living, changing thing. To meet your current goals, you may want to update your strategies.

If loan rates have fallen since you financed your home, now may be the time to renegotiate or *refinance*. Remember that you'll have costs associated with this process, such as application fees, points, and other closing costs that can quickly wipe out any savings you may see from refinancing. Will you be in the home long enough to recoup that money and save over time from the lower interest rate? If not, refinancing isn't for you.

If you do refinance, try to refinance for no more time than it would take to pay off your current mortgage. If you have a 30-year mortgage and have paid 6 years of it, don't get another 30-year mortgage, or you'll end up paying for your house for 36 years. By using the lower interest rate, you can probably pay your current amount, but for a shorter time, such as 20 or 15 years.

 If you choose to pay more than you owe in any month, write a separate check and clearly mark it "for principal only." If you don't specify, the bank will pay itself first — that is, apply the money to interest instead of principal.

In general, your mortgage is the last debt you want to prepay. It probably has a lower interest rate than any other debt on your plate. Additionally, you can deduct mortgage interest from your federal taxable income. In some states, mortgage interest payments are deductible on state income tax returns, as well.

Consolidating Your Bills as a Next-to-Last Resort

If you created your own debt register (refer to Table 5-2), you can see how much you must pay every month just to make the minimum payments on your credit cards and loans. Add your mortgage or rent payment and monthly living expenses, and the total can be overwhelming.

If you can't meet your monthly obligations, no matter how well you budget or how much you can expect to earn from your job(s), you may need a consolidation loan. For this type of loan, the lender pays off all the obligations that you decide to put under the plan. That total is the amount of your loan. You then pay one manageable bill to the lender every month.

Sounds great, doesn't it? The problem is that the interest rate on the consolidation loan is probably as high as that on your *highest* previous debt, and the term is probably longer than that on your *longest* previous debt. Therefore, the cost to you over the term of the loan is much higher than the cost of paying off your debts under their original terms.

 If your consolidation loan is secured by your home — a home equity loan — you can lose your home if you can't make your payments. Some companies specialize in making these types of loans so that they can take possession of the property at the first missed payment. Unlike mortgage lenders that try to help borrowers keep their homes, the purpose of these shark lenders is to profit by taking over property for as little investment as possible.

A consolidation loan looks bad on your credit record. The result may be that in the future, you'll have to borrow at a higher interest rate than if you had paid the debts without consolidating. But a consolidation loan looks a lot better than a default or bankruptcy!

Filing Bankruptcy as a Last Resort

Bankruptcy is the legal cancellation of your debts when you're unable to repay them. Bankruptcy is *not* wiping the slate clean. Although it relieves you of the responsibility for paying past debts, it stays on your credit report for up to ten years, which makes it hard to get credit. Also, you'll pay more — in interest rates, annual fees, application fees, and whatever else lenders can think of — for the credit you can get.

You can get bankruptcy kits at bookstores. Doing so takes time and concentration, but you can fill out the legal papers yourself. If you want to have your papers checked (or you don't even want to attempt an admittedly complicated process), an accountant can do a good job for you at a much lower cost than a lawyer. When you go for help, ask your professional to offer an alternative to bankruptcy — you'll already have gathered the information needed to see whether you can pay off your debts in some way.

 Never use a professional whose sole purpose is to file bankruptcy as opposed to offering good financial advice.

Your papers must be filed with the federal district court for the area in which you live. A court-appointed trustee reviews your application for bankruptcy and recommends to the court whether it should be approved. If your application is not approved, you receive no refund on the fees paid to the court, and you must find a reliable credit counselor to plan a repayment schedule. This is yet another reason to have a professional prepare or review your bankruptcy papers with an eye toward avoiding having to file them at all.

Chapter 6

Saving through Investments

While creating a budget, you discover the multiple benefits of paying off your debts (discussed in depth in Chapter 5), which not only erases the debts themselves but also enables you to stop wasting money by paying interest. Even better, paying off debts releases funds that would have been used to make monthly debt payment and allows you to use them in other areas, like investing. You want to make the most of those "found" dollars and invest them wisely.

This chapter shows you how to determine which types of savings and investment vehicles work for you and your goals. It also shows you how to keep track of the investments in which you decide to put your money.

Identifying Your Saving and Investing Personality

You have a personality that impacts how you go about pursuing your savings and investment goals. Your saving and investing personality reflects how much risk you're willing to take for higher returns.

Risk tolerance is equivalent to an exerciser's tolerance of pain. If you don't believe in pain, you have a *low* risk tolerance — you're willing to accept low interest rates in return for not worrying about your investments. But if you think that you probably need to have a muscle twinge or two to see results, you have a *moderate* risk tolerance — you're willing to take some risk in pursuit of a higher return on investment. If, on the other hand, you believe that

☺ ☹ ☺ ☺ ☺ ☹ ☺ ☺ ☹ ☺ ☺ ☹ ☺ ☺ ☹ ☺ ☺ ☺ ☺ ☹ ☺

if you don't need medical care after your workout, you haven't really worked out, you have a *high* tolerance of risk — you're willing to take big risks in hopes that your investments will grow fast and furiously, and you also feel that you can rebuild your financial foundation if you lose a bundle.

Identify your savings/investment personality in the following list:

❋ **Low risk-taker:** Your primary concern is to conserve your money. People who can't afford to have their nest eggs shrink at all — such as retirees, widows and widowers, and novice and low-income savers — fall into this group.

Low risk-takers depend on savings accounts, certificates of deposit, and other "sure" investments in their portfolios. Worrying about the safety of your investments doesn't keep you up at night if you're a low risk-taker. However, during periods of economic growth, with stable prices but low interest rates, investors in this category can lose ground. Even the most committed low risk-takers must switch some funds to higher-yielding instruments so that inflation doesn't erode their buying power. See the "Understanding Savings and Investment Instruments" section later in this chapter for details.

❋ **Moderate risk-taker:** A moderate risk-taker is more daring than a low risk-taker but is still a conservative investor. Your goals include putting your children through college and planning for retirement. Keeping even with inflation doesn't enable you to reach these goals, however, so you have to take some risk. As a moderate risk-taker, you can afford this risk because you're still in your income-earning years and, by changing your budget, you can make up some of the loss from an investment that has gone bad.

❋ **High risk-taker:** High-risk investors look for large returns on their investments. Sometimes, people who are just starting their careers are high risk-takers because they don't have family responsibilities. Other high-risk investors are speculators who enjoy the thrill of hunting down that big return. Few people fall into this category, because a high risk-taker can lose everything in a single day.

Understanding Savings and Investment Instruments

Savings and investment instruments is just a high-brow way of saying "where you keep your money." The following sections take a look at the most common instruments; those that work for most people. Keep in mind, however, that no savings or investment instrument is right for everyone, and most people have a mix of these investments.

 Your investment portfolio (the group of investments that you hold) may need to reflect some of each type of risk: low, medium, and perhaps even high. This type of investment mixture is called a balanced portfolio. Here, balanced doesn't mean having the same amount in each risk category. Rather, you determine the amount to put in each risk category by taking into account your comfort level and your needs so that your portfolio works for you. A financial planner can help tremendously in this area, as long as he or she understands your risk tolerance.

No one mixture of investments is best for everyone. For example, a low risk-taker needs to conserve capital. The goal is to ensure having a nest egg but to get some higher returns to at least balance the effects of inflation. This person probably wants 50 percent of investments in low-risk investment, perhaps 30 percent in moderate-risk, and 20 percent in high-risk. Someone who is even more fearful of losing his or her nest egg may invest even more conservatively. The investment in low-risk investments may be 60 percent, with 30 percent in moderate-risk and only 10 percent in high-risk.

Savings and money market accounts

Savings accounts and money market accounts are good places to save for short- and mid-term goals, such as buying a new piece of furniture. Because withdrawing your funds from one of these accounts is easy, you can take advantage of special deals as they come up. Banks and credit unions may offer both savings accounts and money market funds, while some mutual fund companies also offer money market accounts.

The main difference between a savings account and a money market account is that your withdrawals are usually limited with a money market account and you may be required to keep a rather large minimum balance (say, $2,500). Before putting money in either type of account, look for the highest interest rate, but make sure no monthly or daily fees apply, so that the cost of doing business with that institution doesn't eat up your interest — or even worse, your principal.

You may be able to set up an automatic monthly deposit into your savings or money market account from your paycheck. To do this, visit your local bank or other financial institution and ask about automatic deposits and transfers. This way, you save regularly without having to physically put the money into your savings account.

 Credit unions and small-town banks are a great way to avoid low balance fees or annual charges charged by some larger banks. The interest rates that credit unions and small-town banks pay on savings accounts and money market accounts are usually comparable to the rates that banks pay.

 If you're a low-risk investor, also consider U.S. savings bonds and other Treasury investments. Your local bank can provide you with all the details on these slow-earning but safe investments.

Certificates of deposit

Certificates of deposit (or CDs) usually earn higher rates of interest than savings accounts do, but they don't charge fees the way mutual funds may (see the "Mutual funds" section later in this chapter). Unlike a savings account, however, you can't add to the deposit or withdraw money before the CD's maturity date without paying a penalty.

The good news with a CD is that you know exactly what to expect and when to expect it. When you purchase a CD, you agree to a certain return in a specified period of time (3 months, 9 months, 18 months, 5 years, and so on), unlike the fluctuating rate of a savings account. Obviously, you want to shop around for the highest rate. And keep in mind that if you cash in your CD before its due date, you have to pay a penalty. For this reason, you don't want to lock in for a long rate if you'll need to use the money before that time.

 If you have a CD that charges a penalty for taking out cash before a certain date and you use this account to pay bills, you are, in effect, throwing money away. Even if you take the money out one day early on a five-year invest- ment, you have to pay a penalty and may also forfeit your interest earnings.

Tax-deferred plans

Tax-deferred plans are great places to put money you plan to use for retire- ment, because you can use pretax dollars. You pay taxes only when you withdraw funds in retirement (when your annual income is likely to be lower than it is now) and, thus, you owe fewer taxes on the investment.

Individual retirement accounts (IRAs), 401(k) plans, annuities, and Keogh plans are voluntary tax-deferred retirement savings plans. They come in many varieties; the type you choose depends on how much you have to invest, where you're employed (whether you work for a small company, large corporation, your own company, or the pubic sector), how much your current income is, and how much income you plan to have in retirement. Because of the wide range of options, see a financial planner or do a thor- ough amount of research before selecting one of these plans.

 401(k) plans are usually managed by your employer. If your employer offers to match your investment (that is, put the same amount into your account that you do), you'll meet you retirement goals twice as fast. Ask your human resources representative for details.

 If you start withdrawing funds from tax-deferred accounts before the age specified (usually 59½ to 65), you must pay a penalty and may forfeit any interest earned.

Mutual funds

A mutual fund pools your money with that of the other investors in the fund and then invests the money on behalf of all the investors. Mutual funds spread out the risk by investing in many companies, stocks, bonds, CDs, and other instruments.

The good thing about mutual funds is that they lower your risk. First, they're managed by professionals, who presumably are able to make wise investment choices. Second, they invest in a range of stocks, bonds, and other vehicles (known as *diversification*), which means that poor performance of some elements is offset by the good performance of others.

 Mutual funds are not appropriate for an investment of less than two years because your return will not cover the fees that you pay.

Choosing a mutual fund may seem daunting, because thousands are available. You can narrow the possibilities by answering the following questions:

* What is your risk-tolerance factor? (See the section "Identifying Your Saving and Investing Personality," earlier in this chapter, if you need help answering this question.)

* Do you want income from your investments, or do you want your earnings to be rolled over for further investment? Choose the appropriate type of account for your needs:

   A *dividends account* is for people who need income to live on.

   A *capital value account* is for people who are trying to maximize the size of their accounts by reinvesting their earnings.

61

☺ ☻ ☹ ☺ ☻ ☹ ☺ ☻ ☹ ☺ ☻ ☹ ☺ ☻ ☹ ☺ ☺ ☻ ☹ ☺

❀ Do you want to invest in domestic, foreign, or mixed companies?

❀ Do you want to pay your management costs when you invest or when you withdraw from the fund?

As you narrow your choices, you'll think of other questions that will guide you to finding the right fund for you.

Analyzing Which Instruments Are Best for You

In choosing a savings or investment instrument, you need to match your goals and your comfort level with three factors:

❀ The interest rate earned

❀ The time frame in which you want to reach your goal(s)

❀ The fees, penalties, and other costs associated with the investment

Interest rates are also known as *rates of return* or *ROR*. When you're receiving interest, you want the highest rate you can get. If the interest is compounded, you want it to be compounded (or rolled over) in the smallest time increments possible because that's how your money grows the fastest.

The time frame is a little bit trickier. For short-term and mid-term goals, such as a new car or a new baby, you want to be able to convert your investment into cash easily and in a short time. However, the longer you commit to an investment, the larger the guaranteed interest rate usually is, so if your time frame is short, you'll likely earn a lower rate of interest than if you could commit to a longer time period. For example, an investment of $1,000 in a 3-month CD may have an annual interest rate of 3.1 percent, whereas a 12-month CD purchased at the same time may have an annual interest rate of 5.5 percent.

For longer-term goals, you can afford a bit more fluctuation. Depending on your needs, you can choose a mutual fund or, if you're not comfortable with that level of risk, choose to put money in your company's 401(k) program. When choosing savings and investment instruments, carefully read the information about fees. Doing so is even more crucial when you're just starting out. For example, if a fund has a fixed fee of $50 per deposit, and you're investing $100,000, the fee is a small price to pay for doing business with that fund (0.05 percent). If you're investing only $1,000, however, $50 is a substantial bite out of your investable dollars (5 percent).

 Never make assumptions about the terms of any of your savings or investment instruments. If changes are made to one of your instruments, read the
new terms and keep the notices on file.

Be sure to consider how your investment decisions impact your income tax
bill. Unlike wages, you control when you pay taxes on your investments by
the types of investments you choose: now (during your higher earning
years) or later (when you retire).

Investing Your Money: The Earlier the Better

Compounding interest is the reason that starting early in your investment
strategy pays off. Because you earn interest not only on your investment
(the *principal*) but also on interest you previously earned, your income
multiplies faster. Compounded interest is one of the reasons that putting
yourself on a tight budget early in your income-earning years pays off later.

Although the amount that you regularly add to your investment fund may
decrease as you pay for a house, raise children, seek more education, care
for your elderly parents, and so on, the money you put in earlier is still
growing. Consider the following example, both at the same rate of interest.

❋ Suppose that, at age 25, Mary Ann invests $2,000 per year for ten
years. Then she stops, and she doesn't put another dime into the
account until she retires. When she turns 65, she'll have $260,690
in the account, even though she invested just $20,000.

❋ Now take a look at Karl, who doesn't start investing until he's 35.
He puts $2,000 per year into an account until he's turns 65. Karl
invests $2,000 per year for 31 years, for a total of $62,000 invested.
Yet at age 65, he has only $228,530 in his account. Although he
deposits $42,000 more into his account than Mary Ann does, he
ends up with $32,160 less at age 65.

By waiting ten years, Karl had to put in more than three times as much
money as Mary Anne, and he still held an investment worth almost 12 percent less than hers.

 You're better off investing a little bit when you're young than waiting until
you're older and investing a lot.

Tracking Your Investments

Tracking is keeping records of how each of your investments is performing. Tracking may take a variety of forms, from simple lists to charts and graphs. People think in different ways, so choose the form that's easiest for you to get quick and clear answers to your questions.

Tracking the performance of your investments keeps you current on trends involving your own investments and in the market as a whole. Efficient investing, like budgeting, relies on good information. To track your data, be sure to read all the information that banks and investment companies send you, keeping track on a separate form.

You can use a simple form like Tables 6-1 through 6-4 to track the performance of your investments. Consider tracking these in pencil, so that you can update them monthly or quarterly or photocopying them and creating new ones each quarter.

Table 6-1 Savings and Money Market Accounts

Date: _____

Bank, credit union, or mutual fund company name	_____
Annual interest rate	_____
Minimum balance	_____
Automatic deposit amounts each month	_____
Current balance	_____

Table 6-2 Certificates of Deposit

Date: _____

Bank or credit union name	_____
Amount of deposit	_____
Annual interest rate	_____
Maturation date	_____
Current balance	_____

☺ ☺ ☹ ☺ ☺ ☹ ☺ ☺ ☹ ☺ ☺ ☹ ☺ ☺ ☹ ☺ ☺ ☹ ☺

Table 6-3 Tax-Deferred Plans

Date: _____

Type of plan _____

Current rate of return _____

Weekly contribution _____

Semi-monthly contribution _____

Monthly contribution _____

Annual contribution _____

Employer matches _____%

Available to withdraw at what age _____

Current balance _____

Table 6-4 Mutual Funds

Date: _____

Fund name _____

Fund type _____

Date purchased _____

Number of shares purchased _____

Purchase price per share _____

Total cost _____

Date shares reinvested _____

Current number of shares _____

Current price per share _____

Current value _____

Dividend paid _____

Date sold _____

continued

Table 6-4 Mutual Funds (continued)

Date: _____

Number of shares sold	_____
Money received	_____
Profit (Loss)	_____
Annual management fees	_____

Going high tech

If you use a personal accounting software package such as Quicken, Budget, or Microsoft Money, keeping track of your investments is even easier. Some of the available features include:

* The ability to track individual investments

* The ability to keep track of entire portfolios

* Graphs showing the history of each of your investments

* Registers showing every transaction for a portfolio

You can create any of these categories on paper, but the software makes record-keeping much easier.

The Internet is also a great source of data on which to make your decisions. You can download financial news, find price updates for instruments in your portfolio, and research historical data about your investments (or ones that you're interested in buying).

Chapter **7**

You Have Your Budget Down Cold, Now What?

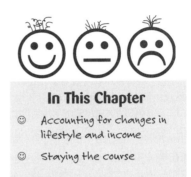

If you're reading this chapter, you've successfully set up a budget, started (or, perhaps, finished) paying down debt, and started saving, and you're well on your way to meeting your financial goals. Doesn't it feel good to know where your money is going? Aren't you enjoying all the energy that you're *not* spending on worrying about money? Isn't it nice to have a picture of your financial future?

When you started on this journey, you spent a lot of time gathering information. Then you had to make decisions — a *lot* of decisions — about the information you gathered. But a budget isn't a static document. As your needs change, so must your budget. This chapter talks about how to maintain and make adjustments to your budget so that you can deal with those changes.

Rebudgeting for Change

You can choose to change your budget either when you're financially uncomfortable or when a major change in your life impacts your financial situation.

What should you do with that raise?

Congratulations: You just got a raise. Of course you want to spend it; that's what a raise is for, right? So, you review your budget to identify likely items to which you may want to apply that new money:

- ❀ Pay down your mortgage early
- ❀ Invest
- ❀ Start a college fund for your children
- ❀ Buy new furniture
- ❀ Go on vacation or upgrade your vacation
- ❀ Contract for maid service

The last three may have surprised you, but remember that you're not supposed to deny yourself everything. You're simply supposed to make a conscious decision about every financial move you make and be aware of the pluses and minuses of each decision.

Explore the maid idea, for example. Do you have a hobby that you'd like to turn into a business, but you're already working full-time? Hiring a maid may free enough time for you to follow your dream. Over the long term, will having a maid allow you to make more money than you pay for her services?

Or maybe you just hate cleaning. It's okay to make a decision just because it's something you want, as long as you know what alternatives you're choosing to do without.

 What you don't want to do is not make a decision. Your money will be gone, and you either won't know where it went or you'll have buyer's remorse because you'll wish that you'd spent it on something else.

You're having a baby!

As happy as the news of a baby on the way is for couples, it's also a cause for panic among the ill-prepared. One of the first questions they may ask is, "How are we going to pay for this?"

Even if the baby is a surprise, you're prepared to reorganize your funds and reprioritize your goals quickly because you have a budget and a savings plan. You know where all your money is going, and you've identified opportunities for cutting more spending or earning extra income. Therefore, you have everything you need to make a good decision about reallocating your funds to meet your new obligations.

Having a baby is more than just hugs and diapers. Using the evaluation skills you've developed by reading this book, you need to make decisions about other changes, such as

☺ ☺ ☹ ☺ ☺ ☹ ☺ ☺ ☹ ☺ ☺ ☹ ☺ ☺ ☹ ☺ ☺ ☺ ☺ ☹ ☺

❋ How are you going to pay the hospital bills? (Or are you going to use a midwife?)

❋ Do you need more insurance?

❋ Do you need larger housing? If not now, when in the future?

❋ How are you going to pay for the ongoing costs of diapers, clothing, food, healthcare, child care, schooling, summer camps, sports, proms, weddings, and all the rest?

And what a lucky baby! From her first allowance, you'll be teaching her the same good budgeting skills that you've learned.

Buying a house

The time has come. You've set up a fund to save for a down payment on a home and have already saved a 20 percent down payment so that you can get the lowest mortgage interest rates. Now you get to make specific decisions about where you'll live: Local real estate offices have forms to help you decide what you want in a house. (Note that your local library may also have plenty of information about home buying.)

The down payment is the biggest struggle in buying a home, but it's only the first piece of the buying puzzle. To avoid unpleasant financial surprises, you also need to make sure that you have enough money to cover the costs of buying, moving into, and owning a home. Table 7-1 provides a form for you to research these costs and plan for them. (Set aside a few hours to call moving companies, utility companies, a local bank or mortgage company, your local tax assessor's office, appliance stores, furniture stores, a home-improvement store, and a home-repair service to get good estimates of these costs.)

Table 7-1 Home-Buying Costs

Expense	Predicted Cost
Moving expenses	
Utility deposits	
Closing costs (points and other fees)	
Monthly mortgage payments	
Property taxes	
Redecorating expense	
Redecorating expense	

continued

Table 7-1 Home-Buying Costs (continued)

Expense	Predicted Cost
New appliance	
New appliance	
New furniture	
Repair expense	

Retaining Your Good Habits

If you've planned well, whatever financial goals you want to reach are now in your budget. If you don't believe that, walk through the following process, one that you probably experience on some level every day.

1 You want to take a three-week trip to Paris.

You have plenty of money in your savings account. Unfortunately, it's not in your vacation savings account, and you don't have enough in your vacation account. You can pay for your flight to and from the City of Light, and can even pay for a hotel. But you don't have enough left to eat, pay admission to the museums, or even ride the Metro. Realizing that you need to regroup, you go on to Step 2.

2 If you take the same amount and stay in Paris for only two weeks, you can eat and see the sights, too.

You won't be able to eat well (in Paris!), and you won't be able to see all the sights, but you'll still have a nice vacation. But you wonder whether a skimpy trip without much in the way of luxuries is what you want. So you survey other choices and go on to Step 3.

3 You consider going to Paris for one week.

Doing so would move enough money from your hotel fund to your food and entertainment fund to give you a first-class vacation. Keep a one-week trip as an option and go on to Step 4.

4 Looking closer to home, you find Montreal, Canada.

They speak French there. They have museums. They have great restaurants and hotels, and you'll save a bundle on airfare.

You now have two alternatives that can meet at least part of your goal. Every choice has a benefit, and you know what that benefit is. Every choice has a negative side, too, and you are aware of that side. Good financial decisions are now at your fingertips.

Chapter 7: You Have Your Budget Down Cold, Now What?

☺ ☺ ☹ ☺ ☺ ☹ ☺ ☺ ☹ ☺ ☺ ☹ ☺ ☺ ☹ ☺ ☺ ☺ ☹ ☺

The habit of making the smart financial planning and spending decisions becomes stronger and stronger as you practice it. Continue to watch your spending throughout your lifetime, noticing your triggers (see Chapter 4), always saving for emergencies (also in Chapter 4), and figuring out ways to meet your financial goals without getting into debt or neglecting important payments (see Chapters 1 through 6). Don't beat yourself up when you do make a financial mistake — after all, you can learn from your mistakes more than your successes — but do stay the course, regardless of the temptations!

Part 3

Getting Down and Dirty with Housecleaning

Housecleaning is a never-ending job. In this part, you find out how to make quick work of your most basic, must-do chores — doing a little bit each day and saving tons of time in the long run. You also get tips for creating custom cleaners to tackle any tough job.

Washing, drying, and ironing your clothes will never be the same, either. I show you how to spend less time ironing, but more time enjoying laundered, pressed clothes. Finally, if you're looking for a fantastic stain removal guide, you've come to the right part.

Chapter **8**

Four Walls and a Floor: Cleaning the Biggest Surfaces

Cleaning walls and floors is time well spent. If either is dingy, your entire room looks unkempt. No matter how much you clean and polish the other items in the room, it will never feel really clean. It's like dressing to the nines without combing your hair or polishing your shoes. You may look okay, but something is marring the finish. With a few steps added to your regular cleaning routine, you can keep walls and floors looking newer longer.

Getting Rid of Dirt on Your Walls

Spots on walls seem to appear mysteriously like they do on your clothes. If you're bothered by a dirty wall, you may think "Why wash? I'll just wait and paint." In reality, washing an entire wall is still much cheaper and faster than painting. But, in most rooms, all you need is some judicious spot cleaning and dusting to keep your walls looking good.

Keep in mind that some paint finishes don't wash well. Flat paints don't tolerate washing well, while gloss, semi-gloss, satin, and eggshell finishes usually wash wonderfully. Some faux finishes don't wash well, because the paint is often diluted and then rubbed on the wall to create the particular effect. Always test on a hidden area first. If you notice that you're rubbing paint off to reveal wallboard or other surfaces in your test spot, you'll likely do the same over the entire surface.

 Look on the label of any leftover paint cans to find out what kind of finishes you have. If you don't have the original cans, go to your local home improvement store and ask someone working in the paint department to show you samples of different finishes to help you determine what you have on your walls.

Washing painted walls, step by step

The most important detail when washing a wall is to control drips by wringing out your sponge or cloth and washing a small area at a time. Follow this simple step-by-step method:

1   **Dust the walls to remove any surface dirt.**

Use a vacuum cleaner or a broom that's covered with a T-shirt or a pair of panty-hose.

2   **Mix up a cleaning solution.**

Use a solution of all-purpose cleaner and water or a light squirt of liquid dish detergent and water in a bucket.

3   **Dunk a 1¹/₂-inch-thick sponge about halfway into the solution.**

Doing so keeps the sponge from getting so saturated that it causes excessive dripping. Wring it out slightly, but leave enough solution to get the wall wet.

4   **Wash a small area at a time.**

Don't make broad, sweeping strokes trying to cover the whole wall at once. Stick to an arm's reach, about a 3-foot-by-3-foot section, overlapping with the preceding area as you go. If you try to do a large area, the wall dries before you have a chance to rinse it off. That practically guarantees streaking.

Squeeze the dirty water out of the sponge as you go. Rinse the wall well, and then move to the next area. If your walls are particularly dirty, you may have to make several changes of water.

5   **After you've covered several sections, wipe the area dry with a clean, absorbent cloth, such as a cloth diaper or towel.**

6   **Don't forget your baseboards.**

They often get dirtier than walls because of shoe scuffs or bumps from the vacuum cleaner. After you've washed the wall, wipe down the baseboard with the same solution and dry it with a cloth.

Making your wallpaper pretty again

Sometimes, you can avoid washing altogether if you give wallpapered walls a good dusting. Vacuum the wallpaper in an upward motion with the brush attachment of your vacuum cleaner. This works great on untreated or *flocked* (a raised fuzzy design) paper and fabric-covered walls. If your vacuum won't reach the ceiling, use the tried-and-true method of tying a T-shirt or pair of pantyhose around a broom and giving the walls a once-over.

 If you still think you have to wash the wallpaper, make sure before you start that the paper is either water-resistant or vinyl-coated and can stand up to washing. Look on the back of any unused rolls of wallpaper or check with the store where you purchased it. Don't wash any untreated wallpaper.

Test the cleaning solution on a hidden section of wall before you start. If the paper isn't damaged, keep going. Wash in the same way as described in the preceding section, using as little water as possible. Too much water near the seams can cause the paper to pull away from the wall.

Clean nonwashable wallpaper with a special dough-type cleaner available at paint stores. Rub the paper with the dough in overlapping strokes, folding as you go to keep exposing clean surfaces of the dough. Always test on a hidden portion of the wall first.

Attacking Stains on Walls

If you clean your walls whenever they need it, your rooms will sparkle for years without repainting or repapering. Sometimes, though, you get an especially bad stain on a wall that makes you think the honeymoon's over. In case some unforeseen glitches occur, use the methods in this section to get common stains off.

Stain solving on washable walls

When treating stains on walls painted with washable paint (check out the "Getting Rid of Dirt on Your Walls" section to determine whether your paint is washable), wash the stain first with a detergent solution. If the stain remains and you want to use an abrasive cleaner, be aware that lots of scrubbing on a wall with an abrasive cleanser will take off some of the paint finish. It's especially noticeable on semi-gloss paint because the sheen will appear flat. You may get the stain off, but you'll also have a big dull spot.

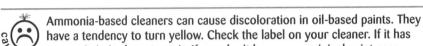
> Ammonia-based cleaners can cause discoloration in oil-based paints. They have a tendency to turn yellow. Check the label on your cleaner. If it has ammonia in it, do not use it. If you don't have your original paint cans to confirm that you don't have oil-based paint on your walls, don't use ammonia-based cleaners. Better safe than sorry.

This list gives you cleaning tips for some troublesome messes that you may encounter:

❀ **Tape:** Lift off the end of the tape by moistening with a dab of oil-free nail-polish remover to soften the glue. Pick up the end and start peeling the tape back slowly and evenly. Then set your hair dryer on low and move it back and forth across the tape as you pull it. After the tape is gone, wash with a detergent-and-water solution.

❀ **Crayon:** Spray the area with a multipurpose spray, such as WD-40, and let it stand for a few minutes. Wipe clean with a soft cloth or paper towel. Then wash the area with a mild solution of liquid dish detergent and water. Rinse with a damp sponge.

Test this on a small hidden area first. Don't use on a wall with flat paint. Use in a well ventilated area away from heat.

❀ **Grease:** First, try wiping it off with a paper towel, and then spraying with a heavy-duty household cleaning detergent. Let the detergent sit for a few seconds, and then rinse and dry. If that doesn't work, try applying a paste of cornstarch and water. Let it dry to a powder, and then vacuum it off.

❀ **Scuff marks:** Try rubbing scuff marks off with an art gum eraser. Or spritz lightly with an all-purpose cleaning solution and rub gently with a plastic scrubber until the stain comes off.

Stain solving on wallpaper

Before you start treating any wallpaper stain, be sure to test the cleaning method on a hidden part of the wall. The following list gives you hints for cleaning some of the most common messes on wallpaper.

❀ **Grease:** Blot the grease with a paper towel. Then place several white paper towels or thick blotting paper over the stain and press the paper with an iron set on low heat. The idea is to make the grease dissolve into the paper. Keep repeating this technique with a clean section of paper until the grease is absorbed. You may have to make several tries.

❀ **Crayon:** Use the same technique as for washable paint in the preceding section. Spot test on a section first. It may be impossible to remove crayon from non-washable paper.

✼ **Fingerprints:** Dirt and grime on fingers can often be a problem especially around light switches. Rub gently with an art gum eraser or a piece of rye bread wadded into a ball.

✼ **Felt-tip pen:** If you're lucky and the pen contains washable ink, wipe the spot with some mild detergent and water. Or spritz with laundry pre-wash spray, rinse, and wipe dry. If that doesn't work, blot the area with a cloth moistened with rubbing alcohol, but test on a hidden area first. Just remember that spots from these pens can spread like crazy, so when you're treating them, blot up the stain very carefully.

Making Floors Fabulous

Keeping your floors clean is not only crucial to the good look of your home but is actually necessary for the longevity of the floor. Hard pieces of dirt left on floors can cause nicks and scratches. Stains and spills can be diffi-cult, if not impossible, to clean if left unchecked. Vacuuming, sweeping, and dust-mopping regularly are the best defense. (Look for electrostatic dust mops, like the Swiffer Sweeper, to make your dust mopping super simple. Always use a dust mop dry — never wet.)

 You can cut down on vacuuming and save wear and tear on your floors by putting throw rugs in high-traffic areas. Popping a throw rug into the wash-ing machine is much easier than cleaning a whole floor.

Getting a handle on dirt

Unless you live in a plastic bubble, dirt will find its way onto your floors. You can minimize its effect by using the following common-sense methods.

✼ **Mat it down.** Put thick mats inside and outside of all entrances and exits to your house. Door mats remove dirt, mud, and grime from the soles of shoes before the dirt can be scattered throughout the house.

✼ **Cover it up.** Before starting any kind of messy project — washing the windows, painting the walls, dyeing your hair, feeding your two-year-old — cover the surrounding area with some kind of protection.

✼ **Blot it off.** Whether a spill happens on a wood floor, linoleum, or carpet, get a paper towel or rag and wipe it up immediately. The longer you procrastinate, the more the spill will seep into the carpet or the floor's finish and possibly become a permanent stain.

Being kind to your wood flooring

Wood floors are beautiful and long lasting, but they usually require more care than other surfaces. You should vacuum and dust-mop at least once a week to remove dust and debris from the seams between the boards and to prevent dirt from being ground into the floor.

 Use the brush attachment on your vacuum cleaner that's meant specifically for hard floors. A canister vacuum with a special bare floor attachment is a good investment if you have lots of wood flooring.

Finishing school for your wood floors

The type of finish on your wood floor determines what kind of care you give it. Three basic types of finishes exist:

✳ **Hard-coat finish:** If your floor has been installed recently, it probably has what's called a *hard-coat finish* — a protective coating that looks like clear plastic on top of the wood. (This is also called a *surface finish*.) The most popular hard-coat finish is polyurethane, but several other treatments look and act the same. All are relatively carefree and never need waxing. This type of finish can scratch, however, so be careful when moving furniture.

To test whether you have a polyurethane-finished floor, dab a few drops of paint remover on a hidden area of the floor like a corner or a closet as the finish will be permanently altered. If the finish bubbles in a few minutes, it's a hard-coat finish.

To clean a hard-coat-finished floor, first sweep or vacuum with a bare-floor attachment, then give it a quick damp-mopping with a mixture of ½ cup white vinegar and 1 gallon water. Dip a sponge mop into the solution, wring it out very thoroughly — it should be about half dry — and then mop a section of the floor. Mop up any drips or puddles. Dry the floor with a clean cloth as you go along.

Never use wax or any oil-based cleaners on a hard-coat finish. If you find a dull spot on the floor, rub it with a clean, soft cloth until the shine comes back.

✳ **Penetrating wax finish:** This type of finish applied as a wax on the surface is absorbed into the wood fibers, which protects the floor from within against dirt, stains, chips, and scratches. It usually has a matte or satin appearance.

If you aren't sure whether your floor has a penetrating wax finish, move your hand across the floor's surface. If you can feel the wood grain, your floor probably has a penetrating finish.

Floors with a penetrating wax finish need to be waxed with a liquid or paste wax at least once a year. The easiest method is to apply a liquid wax, but paste waxes are more durable. Be sure to read the label and buy one that's made for your floor. Using waxes made for resilient (vinyl or linoleum) or tile floors can damage the finish. And don't try to use furniture polish on your floor.

Never soak a wood floor with any liquid.

Protecting the finish of wood floors

Wood floors, like wood furniture, are strong — some have been around for centuries. But because they are porous, wood floors don't react well to excess moisture, extremes of weather, or poor treatment. Take these minor precautions to help keep your wood floors in good shape:

✽ Never saturate a wood floor with water. Water can cause the planks to warp and buckle and stain the finish.

✽ Avoid scratches by putting some kind of covering on the bottoms of chair legs. Try these treatments:

   Coat chair-leg bottoms with a layer of clear nail polish, rub them with floor wax, or glue on felt floor protectors (sold at home-improvement stores).

   When moving a piece of furniture, slip tube socks over the legs or lay old towels underneath them. You can then pull or push the sofa or chair wherever you want and not have to worry about scratches or scuffs on the floor.

✽ To prevent fading or other discoloration due to sunlight, close the curtains or blinds during periods of intense sun or install sheer curtains to block ultraviolet (UV) rays.

Providing disaster relief for waxed wood floors

Accidents will happen, and most can be treated effectively if you hop to it and take immediate action. Table 8-1 addresses some common problems and solutions for waxed floors only: Don't use these methods on any floor with a hard-coat finish.

Table 8-1 Waxed Wood Floor Stains and Common Solutions

Stain	Solution
Alcohol	Rub the spot with liquid or paste wax.
Burns	Rub with extra-fine steel wool dipped in floor cleaner. Wipe dry. Rewax.
Chewing gum, crayon, wax	Harden the area with an ice cube until the gunk is brittle and scrapes off with a dull knife. If debris remains, apply some solvent-based wax around it (but not on it) and allow to soak under the stain to loosen.
Heel marks, scratches	Rub with fine steel wool dipped in floor cleaner. Wipe dry. Rewax.
Oil, grease	Soak cotton with hydrogen peroxide and apply to the stain. Soak a second piece of cotton with plain ammonia and put it on top of the first layer of cotton. Repeat until the stain is absorbed.
Water	Rub the stain with very fine steel wool and rewax. For large stains, lightly sand with fine sandpaper, and then clean with an extra-fine steel wool and mineral spirits or floor cleaner. Refinish and rewax.

Maintaining ceramic tile and resilient (vinyl, asphalt tile, and linoleum) flooring

Most people have some kind of *resilient* floor — vinyl, no-wax vinyl, asphalt tile, linoleum — somewhere in their homes. They are the unglamorous workhorses that seem to look good no matter what you do to them. But they, too, need regular cleaning to keep them in top shape. You can find a wide selection of good commercial cleaners at most grocery stores, discount stores, and home centers.

Be sure to read the label carefully so that you buy the right kind of cleaner for your particular floor. Always test a new cleaner in an inconspicuous area.

To clean a resilient floor, first vacuum the floor before washing it so that you remove any surface dirt. If the floor is only slightly dirty, damp-mop by going over it with a mixture of all-purpose cleaner and water. Be sure to read the cleaner's label to make sure that it works on your type of floor. To damp mop, follow these steps:

1 **Dip the mop into the cleaning solution and wring it out well; it should be damp but not dripping wet.**

2 **Mop a small area at a time (about 3 or 4 feet).**

3 **Rinse and wring the mop frequently.**

Have two buckets handy — one for your cleaning solution and one for clean water. Periodically check the cleaning solution and change it when it becomes too dirty.

4 **Rinse the floor with clean water and wipe it dry with a clean rag.**

Wiping dry rather than air-drying may sound like an unnecessary step, but you get more dirt up in the extra wiping process than you can imagine. The more dirt that comes up now, the longer you can wait until your next cleaning.

Table 8-2 is a useful day-to-day cleaning chart for the ceramic tile and resilient floors in your home.

Table 8-2 Cleaning Chart for Various Non-Wood Hard Floor Surfaces

Surface	To Clean	To Polish	To Fix Scuffs and Heel Marks	Avoid
Ceramic tile, glazed	Vacuum and damp-mop with an all-purpose cleaner; dry with a soft cloth.	Doesn't need polishing	Rub with a plastic scouring pad and non-abrasive cleaner.	Abrasive cleaners.
Ceramic tile, unglazed	Vacuum and damp-mop with an all-purpose cleaner.	Once a year, strip the finish and reseal with a commercial sealer and water-based wax or acrylic self-polishing wax.	Rub with a plastic scouring pad and non-abrasive cleaner.	Abrasive cleaners, strong soaps, or acids.
Linoleum	Vacuum and damp-mop with a mild all-purpose cleaner.	Apply two thin coats of self-polishing, water-based floor wax; let dry between coats.	Rub gently with fine-grade steel wool dipped in liquid floor wax; wipe off with a damp cloth.	Solvent-based products, hot water, and strong soaps.

continued

☺ ☺ ☹ ☺ ☺ ☹ ☺ ☺ ☹ ☺ ☺ ☹ ☺ ☺ ☹ ☺ ☺ ☺ ☺ ☹ ☺

Table 8-2 Cleaning Chart for Various Non-Wood Hard Floor Surfaces (continued)

Surface	To Clean	To Polish	To Fix Scuffs and Heel Marks	Avoid
Vinyl	Vacuum and damp-mop with an all-purpose cleaner dissolved in water.	Apply two thin coats of self-polishing, water-based floor wax; let dry between coats.	Scrub lightly with a synthetic scouring pad floor wax; wipe with a damp towel.	Abrasive cleaners.
Vinyl, no-wax	Vacuum and damp-mop with an all-purpose cleaner recommended for no-wax floors.	Surface should have a permanent shine, but if it becomes dull in high-traffic areas, apply a commercial gloss-renewing product.	N/A	Solvent-based products or cleaners with pine oil, strong soap, hot water, or abrasives.

Keeping your carpet clean

Keeping your carpet clean actually extends the life of the carpet. Dirt can break down carpet fibers quickly. In addition, the deeper the dirt gets into the fibers, the harder the dirt is to remove. Regular weekly cleaning (more often in high-traffic areas) is the optimum way to keep your carpet clean and healthy.

Vacuuming 101

Before you start to vacuum, declutter the area so you don't have to start and stop while working. Go around the room and pick up toys, coins, paper clips, safety pins, rubber bands, and other small objects that can clog the vacuum. (This is a good job for kids to do.)

If you're working on a large room, don't try to vacuum the whole width and length at once. Break the room into small sections so that you can easily keep track of what you've done. Getting your rug really clean takes time. Go slowly over each section, several times, moving the vacuum back and forth in overlapping strokes. A quick once-over won't do it!

Staying on top of spots and spills

Stains and spills are going to happen. That's a fact of life. You can forbid everyone to eat in the living room, and you can make family and friends take off their shoes, but eventually, someone or something is going to slip and splat. And then you've got a spot.

In your anxiety to treat the spill quickly, however, you need to recognize the following don'ts:

❀ **Don't use colored cloths or towels to wipe up a spot.** The liquid in the spill can make any colored dyes in the cloth bleed onto the carpet and cause a new stain.

❀ **Don't rub or scrub the spot.** Thinking that the more you rub, the better you clean is a natural reaction. Rubbing and scrubbing can force the spill further into the fibers of the carpet and make it more difficult to clean.

❀ **Don't pour cleaning fluid on the spot.** It can spread the stain and damage the backing of the carpet. Use a spray bottle or blot it with a clean cloth.

❀ **Don't remove the cleaning solution immediately.** Let it sit on the spot for 5 to 10 minutes. Then start blotting.

Stockpile the following essentials in a carryall tray or basket for the day when disaster strikes, and you'll be able to bound into action faster than a speeding bullet:

❀ Several thick, absorbent, white cloths, such as towels, washcloths, or cloth diapers (my favorite!)

❀ Liquid dishwashing detergent

❀ Dry-cleaning solvent available at hardware or department stores.

❀ Spray bottle filled with a mixture of ¼ teaspoon liquid dishwashing liquid and 1 cup water

❀ Spray bottle of clear water for rinsing

❀ White vinegar

❀ Plain ammonia

❀ Nail polish remover, nonacetone

❀ Spoon or old credit card to scrape up solid spills

Table 8-3 lists common spots and suggested removal strategies. Follow the strategies in order of the steps given, starting with the first suggested spot removal solution (Step 1) and continuing with subsequent step until you see improvement. If that doesn't work, go on to the next step. Remember, keep trying. If the stain remains, call a professional.

85

☺ ☺ ☹ ☺ ☺ ☹ ☺ ☺ ☹ ☺ ☺ ☹ ☺ ☺ ☹ ☺ ☺ ☺ ☺ ☹ ☺

Table 8-3 Spot Removal Chart for Carpets

Spill	Solution				
	Step 1	Step 2	Step 3	Step 4	Step 5
Alcohol	Detergent solution	Ammonia solution	White vinegar solution	Warm water rinse	Call a pro
Candy	Detergent solution	Ammonia solution	White vinegar solution	Warm water rinse	Call a pro
Chocolate	Dry-cleaning fluid	Detergent solution	Ammonia solution	White vinegar	Warm water rinse
Coffee with cream and sugar	Dry-cleaning fluid	Detergent solution	White vinegar solution	Warm water rinse	Spot removal kit
Crayon	Dry-cleaning fluid	Detergent solution	Call a pro		
Egg	Detergent solution	Ammonia solution	White vinegar solution	Warm water rinse	Call a pro
Glue, household	Detergent solution	White vinegar solution	Warm water rinse	Spot removal kit	Call a pro
Grape juice	Detergent solution	White vinegar solution	Warm water rinse	Spot removal kit	Call a pro
Greasy food	Dry-cleaning fluid	Detergent solution	Warm water rinse	Call a pro	
Markers, felt tip	Detergent solution	Warm water rinse	Call a pro		
Salad dressing	Dry-cleaning fluid	Detergent solution	Spot removal kit	Warm water rinse	Call a pro
Spaghetti sauce	Detergent solution	Ammonia solution	Warm water rinse	Call a pro	
Wine	Detergent solution	White vinegar solution	Ammonia solution	Warm water rinse	Spot removal kit

To make these spot-removal solutions, use the following concentrations recommended by the Carpet and Rug Institute. Don't use anything stronger or you run the risk of damaging your carpet.

❋ **Detergent solution:** Mix $1/4$ teaspoon dishwashing liquid (clear, non-bleach, non-lanolin) with 1 cup warm water. After you apply the solution, let it sit on the stain for 8 to 10 minutes and then rinse thoroughly until all the detergent disappears.

❋ **White vinegar solution:** Mix 1 cup white vinegar with 2 cups water.

❋ **Ammonia solution:** Mix 2 tablespoons household ammonia with 1 cup water.

❋ **Dry-cleaning fluid:** Use a nonflammable solution, such as Carbona Stain Devils or K2R. Put the dry-cleaning fluid on a cloth or sponge — not directly on the carpet, which could destroy the backing.

   If you can't find dry-cleaning fluid, you can also use nail-polish remover. Use one that doesn't contain acetone (read the label) and treat in the same manner as dry-cleaning fluid. Those containing amyl acetate can be used, but they leave a residue that can cause rapid soiling.

❋ **Spot-removal kit:** Available at carpet and department stores, these kits contain a stain-resistant solution that's applied after the detergent solution that's also in the kit. Be careful not to apply the stain-resistant solution before the spot is completely removed, or the stain could become permanent. Also available for most common household spots are dry extraction cleaning compound kits. Follow the directions carefully on both kits.

The Carpet and Rug Institute suggests taking the following steps for getting rid of most spots. Remember to act fast, scraping up solids and blotting up liquids. To absorb the liquid, cover the area with several white paper towels and weight them down with a heavy, flat object (books or magazines may fade into the carpet). Replace the paper towels and continue this process until all the moisture is absorbed.

1   Pretest any spot removal solution on a hidden portion of the carpet to see whether it damages the fibers or dye.

   To pretest the solution, put a few drops of cleaner on each color of the carpet, and hold a clean cloth or towel on the area for 10 seconds. Check whether any dyes from the carpet bled onto the cloth or whether the carpet appears changed in any way.

   If you see any change, try another cleaning solution or call a professional.

2   Apply a few drops of the first suggested cleaning solution from Table 8-3, let sit for 5 to 10 minutes, and blot gently.

   Work from the edges of the spill to the center to prevent the spill from spreading. Keep blotting and applying the cleaning solution until no more of the spill transfers to the cloth. This may require several tries.

☺ ☺ ☹ ☺ ☺ ☹ ☺ ☺ ☹ ☺ ☺ ☹ ☺ ☺ ☹ ☺ ☺ ☹ ☺

3   If you no longer see any improvement, rinse with warm water, blot, and then go to the next solution listed in Table 8-3 and repeat Steps 1 and 2.

If you need to try two or three different cleaning solutions on the same spot, use in the order suggested in Table 8-3 and be sure to rinse well between each step.

After you've removed the spill, rinse the area thoroughly with a spray bottle of water or a dab of water on a clean cloth. Don't pour on water when rinsing; you don't want moisture in the floor or padding. After applying water, press down on the area with an absorbent cloth to soak up all the cleaning solution.

If you've tried all the suggested solutions and nothing works, throw in the towel and call a professional rug cleaner. For other carpeting questions, call the Carpet and Rug Institute at 800-882-8846 or go to its Web site at www.carpet-rug.com.

Removing tough stains

Pet stains, burns, smells, and other special carpet problems are really tough (but not impossible) stains to remove:

✸ **Animal messes:** Blot liquid messes with a towel and scrape off solids with a spoon. Flush with lukewarm water, and then apply a mixture of equal parts white vinegar and water. Again, blot the liquid until it's dry. If the spot remains, apply a solution of $1/4$ teaspoon dishwashing liquid and 1 cup water. Blot again. Reapply the vinegar solution and let it sit for 5 minutes. Then blot the excess liquid with several towels, replacing the towels until all the moisture is removed. For several pet messes, use an enzymatic cleaner from a pet store. Follow the label instructions and test on a hidden area first.

✸ **Chewing gum:** Put an ice cube in a plastic bag and hold it on top of the gum to harden it. Pick at the gum and pull off as much as you can very carefully so that you don't pull up any carpet fibers. Dot with methyl salicylate (Extra-Strength Ben-Gay) and gently pull the rest off. After the gum is removed, clean the area with a detergent solution, followed by a warm water rinse.

✸ **Ink:** Pour a small amount of rubbing alcohol (90 percent isopropyl) on a cloth. Dot the stain carefully, following the previously mentioned stain removal steps in the preceding section, and then blot. Don't pour alcohol directly on the stain or rub the stain — that can cause ink to spread. And believe me, when ink spreads, there's no stopping it.

Taking care of burns and other problems

Your carpet can be marred by more than spills and stains. Even having your furniture sit on the carpet for long periods of time can cause problems. The following list provides solutions to the most common concerns:

❀ **Burns:** For a small burn from a cigarette or a match, carefully clip off any blackened tufts in the rug, using small, sharp scissors. Trim the fibers around the immediate area very slightly so the indentation won't show so much. If you have a small area that's burned down to the backing, you can try repairing it.

Using a utility knife and a metal ruler, cut a square patch of carpeting slightly larger than the burned area from a carpet remnant or hidden area like a closet floor. Center the patch over the burned area and cut a piece of the area the same size as the patch. Be careful not to cut through the pad. Remove the damaged piece and check to make sure the new patch fits. Line the outside of the hole with double-stick carpet tape. Lightly apply fabric glue to the edges of the patch, and then place the patch into the hole. After the glue sets, fluff up the fibers between the patch and the surrounding carpet to blend them in. If the burn is large, call a professional to replace that area of carpet.

❀ **Dents:** Dents occur when furniture stays in one place for a long time. Prevent this problem by periodically repositioning your furniture around the room. Moving it slightly will do the trick. To fix a dent, brush the area with your fingertips to loosen and gently pull up the tufts. Wait a couple of days, and if the depression still exists, mist the area with warm water. Hold a hair dryer set at low over the area and lift the pile with your fingertips while you move the dryer back and forth over the spot.

❀ **Fading:** The color of a carpet or rug can fade if the carpet is continually exposed to strong sunlight. Your best defense is to draw the curtains during the day when the sun is at its brightest. (Dyed nylon or olefin carpets resist fading better than other fabrics.)

❀ **Carpet odors:** Sprinkle a dry carpet with baking soda, wait 15 minutes, and then vacuum. (Test on a hidden corner first.) Or use a commercial odor remover.

❀ **Snags:** A loose carpet thread that has pulled away from the carpet is known as a *snag.* Clip it off carefully with small scissors so that it's level with the rest of the carpet.

Doing the big clean

Every 12 to 18 months, have your carpets deep-cleaned. You have three basic methods to choose from (use the method recommended by the carpet manufacturer to maintain the warranty if it's still valid):

❀ **Dry extraction:** A dry compound is brushed on the rug, the soil is absorbed into the compound, and the carpet is vacuumed.

❀ **Rotary shampoo:** A neutral detergent, made just for carpet, is applied to the carpet. Be sure to rinse and extract all the moisture.

❀ **Water extraction:** A cleaning solution is injected into the pile and then extracted. The extraction of every bit of moisture is important.

The easiest to do yourself is the dry extraction method, but you can rent equipment and do the rotary shampoo or water extraction methods yourself. Just be sure to follow the manufacturer's directions for the equipment and apply the solutions carefully. Don't use more than the suggested amount of shampoo solution and minimize the amount of water used. Residue left on carpet can cause faster resoiling.

 If you choose to have your carpet professionally cleaned, do a little research before you choose a service. Ask your friends for recommendations or ask the store where you purchased your carpet. Have the service come to your home to make an estimate. Get everything in writing. After you decide on a company, check with the Better Business Bureau (BBB) to see whether any complaints have been filed against it.

Chapter 9

Knick Knacks, Grab Some Stacks, Make Those Chair Arms Shine

You hate to clean. You, too, huh? Cleaning can be frustrating, time-consuming, and, well, just plain dirty work. You clean one day, and then, seemingly from nowhere, dust and grime reappear.

But, like failing to floss your teeth, dust and dirt can wreak havoc if ignored. A couple-minute task can turn into a full-scale attack with scrub brushes, heavy-duty cleaners, and hours of hard labor. In this chapter, you find out how to make quick (and regular) work out of these tedious, but essential chores. You discover how to simplify some common (and some of the toughest) cleaning chores. You also get tips on caring for your furniture and other treasures.

The Dust-Busters: Dusting Tools

Clean cloths are the number-one dust-busting tool. The best dust cloths are lint free and 100-percent cotton, so recycle those no-longer-wearable light-colored T-shits, cotton flannel pajamas, and old linen napkins. Cut them into a size that's large enough to fold a couple of times and hold comfortably in your hand. That way, you can dust on one side and then turn to the other side and refold for more dusting.

Lambswool duster

A long fluffy tube of lambswool on a stick is a favorite of professional cleaners because it attracts and holds dust. Try to get one that has a

☺ ☺ ☹ ☺ ☺ ☹ ☺ ☺ ☹ ☺ ☺ ☹ ☺ ☺ ☹ ☺ ☺ ☺ ☹ ☺

handle that can be extended to ceiling height so that you can clean chandeliers and ceiling corners without having to get up on a ladder. After you're finished using the duster, take it outside and shake it or bang it against the bottom of your shoe until the dust comes off.

The versatile vacuum cleaner

The vacuum is an under-appreciated cleaning tool. You may think of it as useful only when cleaning carpets, but with just a few attachments (see Figure 9-1), your vacuum can help you speed-clean the whole house. The most commonly used attachments include the following:

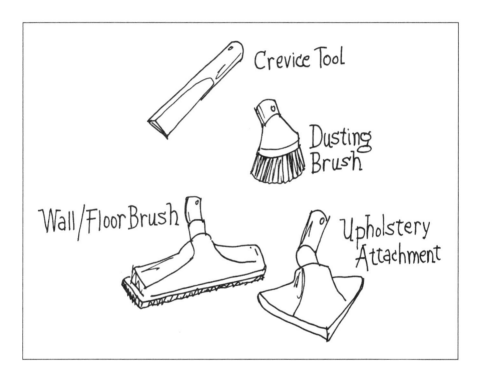

Figure 9-1: Some useful vacuum cleaner attachments.

❋ **Crevice tool:** Picks up dirt from wicker furniture, wall heaters, windows and window sills, heating ducts, air conditioner filters, and furniture crevices.

❋ **Dusting brush:** Also cleans along baseboards, shelves, top of door frames, window sills, piano keys, carved furniture, picture frames, and door moldings.

☺ ☺ ☹ ☺ ☺ ☹ ☺ ☺ ☹ ☺ ☺ ☹ ☺ ☺ ☹ ☺ ☺ ☺ ☹ ☺

- ❀ **Upholstery tool:** Sucks out dust from upholstery and can also be used for draperies, mattresses, and carpet stairs.

- ❀ **Wall/floor brush:** Gets surface dirt off walls, non-carpeted floors, and ceilings.

Dusting 101

The basic idea behind dusting is to pick up the dust and remove it — not just move it around or fling it into the air. The simplest method is to spray a very light spritz of water or a dusting product, like Endust on a cloth, because dirt will cling to the cloth like magic. Just make sure you spray liquid on the cloth, not on the item you're cleaning.

To make your dusting life exponentially easier, try dry electrostatic dusting cloths available at just about any discount or grocery store. Common brand names for these products include, Swiffer and Pledge Grab-Its. They grab and hold dust, and, thanks to their electrostatic properties, they also repel future dust. Their convenience continues because you can toss the cloths in the trash when you're finished.

Table 9-1 presents some common dust collectors you may have in your house, along with some methods for cleaning them.

Table 9-1 Daily Dusting How-To's

Item	By Hand	By Machine (Vacuum Cleaner Attachment)
Blinds (mini or venetian)	Lambswool dusting tool or cotton gloves	Dusting brush
Computer screen	Wipe with soft cloth	Soft dusting brush or tiny minivacs designed for the purpose
Computer keys	Wipe with a soft cloth from the center out	Dusting brush
Dresser drawers	Move everything to one side, wipe with cloth	Crevice attachment
Books	Lambswool dusting wand or socks	Dusting brush
Framed posters, pictures	Soft cloth very lightly misted with glass cleaner	Soft dusting brush

continued

☺ ☻ ☹ ☺ ☻ ☹ ☺ ☻ ☹ ☺ ☻ ☹ ☺ ☻ ☹ ☺ ☺ ☻ ☹ ☺

Table 9-1 Daily Dusting How-To's *(continued)*

Item	By Hand	By Machine (Vacuum Cleaner Attachment)
Leather furniture	Wipe with a soft cloth or old socks	Dusting brush
Pleated lampshade	Paintbrush or hair dryer	Dusting brush
Radiator	Old sock on the end of a yardstick	Crevice tool
Shutters	Foam brush or old socks	Dusting brush
Sofa	Whisk broom	Upholstery attachment
Telephone	Soft cloth misted with all-purpose cleaner	Dusting brush
Wood surfaces	Soft cloth sprayed with dust control spray (like Endust)	Dusting brush

Everything in life has a natural order, and this applies to dusting, as well. The rule is: Dust from the top down. The reason is simple — gravity.

Because dirt falls onto the floor when you're dusting, you also want to vacuum after you're finished. (This makes dusting easier, too, because you don't worry about all the dust that's falling to the floor.) Just be sure to save your vacuuming for the final pickup.

 Dust and vacuum on rainy or humid days. The dampness keeps the dust from rising and floating. If you're sweeping dust into a dustpan, moisten the pan slightly to keep the dust from floating out of the dustpan and into the air.

Taking Care of Wood Furniture

Knowing the finish on your furniture is key to giving it proper care. The easiest way to determine whether your furniture has an oil finish or a lacquer finish is to apply a dab of boiled linseed oil to a cloth and rub it on.

✽ If the oil disappears and is absorbed into the finish, you have an *oiled* (or *soft*) *finish.*

✽ If the oil's not absorbed and instead beads up like drops of water on glass, you have a *hard* (or *lacquered*) *finish.*

When you're done with this test, wipe off the oil. Don't panic if the finish momentarily darkens. The oil will eventually be absorbed into the wood.

Boiled linseed oil is available in hardware stores, already labeled as "boiled." Never boil or heat it up at home.

Polishing different finishes

After you determine what type of finish your furniture has (see the preceding section), select a polish or wax made specifically for that type of finish and test it on a hidden area. Read all the product information on the bottle. After you find a product that you like, stick with it. Applying one polish on top of another brand can sometimes dull the finish.

 Whether your finish is oiled or lacquered, never apply polish or wax directly to the wood. Always apply it first to a soft, lint-free cloth and then use that cloth on the wood. Also, never apply polish or wax without dusting first to avoid grinding in the dust and embedding it in the finish.

Caring for oiled (soft) finishes

Many polishes for oil finishes are available commercially. Regularly clean furniture with oiled finishes by using a lightly dampened cloth to remove dust. Once a year, apply boiled linseed oil or some comparable product in a well-ventilated area to replenish the natural sheen of the finish and to prevent the wood from drying out. Never apply wax to an oiled (or soft) finish because doing so can damage the surface.

Polishing and cleaning hard (lacquered) finishes

With lacquered finishes, dust about once a week with a soft cloth slightly dampened with a dust spray. Every eight weeks or so, apply a wax polish appropriate for your type of finish. Polish in the direction of the grain and buff with a clean cloth to avoid build-up of the polish.

 Hand wash and air-dry any cloths used for polishing and waxing furniture. Never put them in the washer and dryer. They can leave a harmful residue in the washer and are flammable in the heat of the dryer.

Protect surfaces that get a lot of wear, such as the arms of chairs and rockers, by polishing them more frequently.

Fixing spots and stains on wood finishes

You don't want your furniture to be marred by spots and stains. As a preventive measure, use trivets and coasters whenever possible and wipe up all spills immediately. Just as too much dryness and heat is bad for wood, so is too much moisture.

If you end up with unsightly marks anyway, use the solutions in this section to take care of problems.

✲ **Burn marks:** If you have a light burn, try mixing a paste of finely powdered pumice (available at most hardware stores) with boiled linseed oil. Use a soft cloth and gently rub it on in the same direction as the wood's grain. Repeat this procedure as necessary.

✲ **Candle wax:** Most wax can be removed by lifting it carefully. Use something stiff but still fairly soft to pry the wax up from the furniture. A piece of cardboard, a credit card, or a plastic pastry scraper all work great, but be sure to use them gently. If the wax still doesn't budge, try waving a hair dryer set on low over the spot to soften it, but don't let the dryer get hot enough or close enough to melt the wax. If a mark remains, rub the area with extra-fine steel wool dipped in mineral spirits, and then wipe dry.

✲ **Scratches and cracks:** Most scratches can be wiped away with a good polishing or can be buffed out with wax. For deeper scratches, you can purchase specially made wax fill-in sticks at a hardware store or home improvement center for this purpose.

✲ **Stuck-on paper:** Just pour some vegetable oil onto a cloth and dampen the paper thoroughly. Wait about five minutes and rub along with the grain using a cloth, or try extra-fine steel wool. Wipe dry.

✲ **Water spots, white heat marks, and crayon marks:** Wipe a small amount of mayonnaise on any of these stains, let sit a couple of minutes, and then remove with a clean cloth. Or try leaving a small dab of petroleum jelly on a water spot overnight. Wipe it away in the morning.

Caring for Upholstered Furniture

An undusted cushion or piece of upholstered furniture isn't as innocent as it may seem. Even if you can't see it, the dust is there, building up day after day. Besides the fact that dirt is piling up inside the cushions, allergy sufferers may react to the dust particles and dust mites that live in upholstered furniture.

To keep your house clean, vacuum your upholstered furniture with the upholstery attachment at least once a week, more often if someone in your house suffers from allergies. Use the crevice tool, a long and thinly tapered attachment, to vacuum along seams and into crevices and hidden corners. When you're finished cleaning, rotate your sofa cushions, just as you do your tires, so that they wear evenly.

If you spill something on the fabric, blot it up immediately. Even if your upholstered furniture has been treated with fabric protector, you must still clean up mishaps promptly. Fabric-protecting treatments are stain-resistant, not stain-proof. The furniture industry has developed a "cleanability" code that's helpful when you're trying to figure out how to clean your upholstered furniture. They suggest what type of cleaner to use for the fabric of your furniture. See Table 9-2 to break the code:

Table 9-2   Upholstery Cleaning Codes

Code	What It Means
W	Use a water-based cleaner
S	Use a water-free dry-cleaning solvent
WS	Use either a water-based or solvent-based cleaner
X	None of the preceding cleaners can be used. Clean fabric only by vacuuming, light brushing, or professional cleaning.

So that you're not tearing apart your furniture, looking for codes in an emergency, fill in Table 9-3 with the cleaning codes on your furniture. Check the underside of cushions or the back of your furniture for these codes.

Table 9-3   Your Upholstered Furniture's Cleaning Codes

Item	Code	Last Cleaned	Comments
Couch			
Love seat			
Arm chair			
Recliner			
Chaise lounge			
Dining room chairs			
Bar stools			
Office chair			
Bedroom chair			

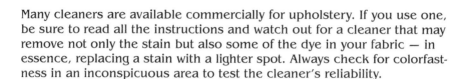
Many cleaners are available commercially for upholstery. If you use one, be sure to read all the instructions and watch out for a cleaner that may remove not only the stain but also some of the dye in your fabric — in essence, replacing a stain with a lighter spot. Always check for colorfastness in an inconspicuous area to test the cleaner's reliability.

After any upholstery treatment, remember to vacuum the furniture thoroughly to remove any detergent or cleaner residue that could attract more dirt. For a really deep and thorough cleaning, rent a professional steam extraction machine. This machine actually forces the cleaner into the fabric, while sucking it back out again — very similar to a steam carpet cleaner.

Cleaning Leather and Wicker Furniture

Casual, easy-care furniture is extremely popular, both indoors and out. From leather sofas to wicker furniture, people are entertaining and living in every room of their houses. While casual furniture is, by definition, easy to care for, some care is still involved. This section tells you how to keep casual furniture clean.

Leather furniture

Although leather is relatively carefree, you should dust and vacuum your leather furniture regularly with the upholstery attachment of your vacuum. If it needs a deeper cleaning, wipe it off with saddle soap, but be sure to check the leather manufacturer's care label first. Use as little water as possible.

 If the leather starts to feel and look dry, rub it with some white petroleum jelly or castor oil. Never wax it. Leather won't absorb wax. Wipe off any excess jelly or oil with a clean cloth.

Wicker, bamboo, and cane furniture

Wicker, bamboo, and cane furniture needs to be dusted and vacuumed regularly, using the soft brush attachment of your vacuum. Be careful that you don't pull up any splintering edges.

Wash these materials with a mild, sudsy detergent, such as Murphy's Oil Soap. Use as little water as possible to get them clean and use a soft brush to really get into the edges. When you're finished cleaning, rinse with clean water and dry thoroughly. Unlike wood furniture, wicker, bamboo, can, rush, and sea grass furnishings actually benefit from a little moisture, so give them a damp wipe with a clean cloth occasionally.

☺ ☺ ☹ ☺ ☺ ☹ ☺ ☺ ☹ ☺ ☺ ☹ ☺ ☺ ☹ ☺ ☺ ☺ ☹ ☺

Cleaning Chandeliers, Candlesticks, and Other Stuff

Every household has a variety of items that need to be cleaned. Some are delicate, like chandeliers. Others just seem to live to catch dust, like baskets and books. Still others are well-used and can take a pounding. The following list includes some of the most common miscellaneous cleaning tasks:

✽ **Baskets:** For day-to-day cleaning, brush out dust with a stiff paintbrush or clean with the brush attachment of your vacuum cleaner. Clean with warm water and a mild soapy solution like Murphy's oil soap and a soft cloth. Rinse thoroughly, dry off with a terry cloth towel, and air dry before putting it away.

✽ **Candlesticks:** Wax drippings are easier to remove if you place the candlestick in the freezer for an hour to shrink the wax before you peel it off. Or soak the candlestick in hot water (except wood) and rub lightly, rinsing in hot water. To keep candlestubs from sticking, put a couple drops of water in the bottom of the candleholder before inserting the candle.

✽ **Chandeliers:** Dust periodically with a lambswool duster or blow off the dust with a hair dryer set on low heat. Before you clean the chandelier, however, turn it off and let the bulbs cool. Cover the floor underneath with several thicknesses of newspaper or towels to catch any drips and to cushion any *prisms* (the small crystals that dangle from crystal chandeliers) that may fall. Spray the prisms with window cleaner or with a homemade solution of 2 teaspoons rubbing alcohol and a pint of distilled water. Put on a pair of soft white cotton gloves and gently rub each prism dry.

✽ **Eyeglasses:** If your eye-care specialist recommends a particular cleaning solution and cloth, use both. This is particularly true if you have a special type of coating on your glasses. Otherwise, dip your glasses in a solution of mild dishwashing detergent and water, and then wipe with a soft cloth. Rinse off in clear water and blot dry with a soft cloth. Avoid wiping the glass dry; small particles of dirt can scratch the glass.

✽ **Fans:** Unplug portable fans and turn of ceiling fans before cleaning. Spray the blades of ceiling fans with all-purpose household cleaner and wipe off with a damp cloth. Use a long-handled duster to dust the blades regularly. Vacuum the dust off the *grilles* (the grating on the front and back of a portable fan) with a brush attachment on your vacuum cleaner. Dust the blades inside by blowing the dust off with a hair dryer set on low. If you can take off the grilles, clean the blades with household cleaner and a damp cloth.

☺ ☺ ☹ ☺ ☺ ☹ ☺ ☺ ☹ ☺ ☺ ☹ ☺ ☺ ☹ ☺ ☺ ☺ ☹ ☺

❀ **Fireplace glass doors:** Spray the cool glass with a commercial glass cleaner or a mixture of ¼ cup vinegar, 1 tablespoon ammonia, and 1 quart water. Wipe off with a soft lint-free cloth.

❀ **Picture frames:** The glass on the frame can be cleaned by wiping with a cloth dampened with window cleaner. Never spray the glass itself; it could seep behind the frame and damage the artwork. Clean wood frames by rubbing with a cloth dampened with a couple of drops of wood oil.

Chapter **10**

The Busiest Rooms in the House: The Kitchen and Bath

You may not use your living room or dining room every single day, but your kitchen and bath get a daily workout. Even with the most modern appliances and care-free surfaces, these rooms still aren't self-cleaning. All the dust and dirt that sneaks into other rooms also gathers here, but so do the dishes from everyone's meals and the debris of cleaning your family's bodies, from head to toe.

Kitchen and Bath Cleaning Basics

You can get away with not cleaning the living room and bedroom for days, maybe even for weeks, but if you don't clean the kitchen on a daily basis, it's chaos. But like everything else, if you're smart about the way you cook and clean, your kitchen will sparkle without much effort. And quick daily touchups in the bathroom keep your sinks, toilets, and showers in company-ready mode anytime.

Keeping the kitchen clean while you work

If you're careful while you cook and adopt some cook-'n'-clean policies, you can keep the mess in check and eliminate a nightmare clean up after each meal. Here are some simple tips.

❋ **Choose the right size pan for the job.** If you're baking food with lots of liquid, make sure the sides of the pan are high enough to prevent spills when you lift it out of the oven.

❋ **Because water causes grease to bubble up and spray on walls, make sure all food is as dry as possible before putting it in the frying pan.** Pat dry foods that you've rinsed or defrosted. If oil starts to bubble up, invert a colander over the pan to stop the spatters.

❋ **Put a washable floor mat in the area where you have the most spills.** Cleaning the mat is easier than cleaning the whole floor.

❋ **Use a large pan when cooking foods such as pasta, rice, milk, and dried beans, which have a tendency to boil over easily.** Always keep an eye on the stove so you can immediately take care of any mishaps.

A few minutes spent preparing your kitchen area to prevent and avoid clean-up problems can save you hours of heavy clean-up time later and keep your kitchen looking nice while you cook.

Daily bathroom duties

Make sure each person in the family is assigned to clean up after his or her shower: A quick rinse of the stall with the showerhead is all it takes, followed by a swipe with a squeegee or paper towel. Bath people (as opposed to shower people) aren't off the hook, either: After a bath, quickly wipe the bottom and sides of the tub with a sponge and then rinse with spray from the shower.

Quickly remove spots from mirrors by wiping the spot with a damp paper towel and buffing with a dry one.

Baby wipes are an excellent product to use for spot cleaning the bathroom, because they're pre-moistened and you don't have to rinse. Use them on sinks, faucets, toilets, and even non-wood floors for a quick touch up anytime.

Keeping your favorite products nearby

Keep your products close to where you use them. It's much easier to clean daily when you don't have to trek upstairs or downstairs to get the job done.

Cleaning Cabinets, Counters, Floors, and Faucets

Even though most of the surfaces in the kitchen and bath are designed to stand up to daily use, they still need diligent care to keep them clean and looking good. Some are more delicate than others.

 If you have any doubt about how to clean a surface, test the cleaning fluid or brush or pad on a hidden area first. If it leaves any unwanted mark, switch to something else.

Cabinets: Start with the handles

Most of the cabinet cleaning you'll have to do is around the handles, where dirty hands reach out and touch everyday. If you keep the handle areas clean, you can go for quite a while without washing the entire cabinet. Use a cotton swab or a toothbrush dipped in cleaning solution for the narrow areas around the handle. Wipe up any smudges or spots with household cleaner and a sponge as soon as they occur.

Keep cabinet shelves clean by lining them with washable shelf liner. For small spills, simply wash off the paper. When the shelf gets really dirty, you just change the liner. Voilà — shelves are clean!

Countertops

Keeping the countertops clean is important not only for good looks but also for sanitary reasons, because bacteria from uncooked food are available to contaminate other surfaces and other foods if you're not careful.

Clean daily grime and most spills with an all-purpose household cleaner. Stubborn spots can be removed with a paste of baking soda and water. If you're using oven or drain cleaner in the area, don't put it on the countertop, or you may mar its finish.

 Always use cutting boards when doing any kind of kitchen task. Not only do cutting boards keep the countertop free from cuts and scratches, but spills and stains are easier to clean off of the cutting board than the countertop. And you can use separate cutting boards for different foods. Plastic or acrylic cutting boards are more sanitary than wooden ones, because they don't absorb meat and other juices.

Laminate and cultured marble counters

Laminate (with names like Formica and Wilsonart) is a waterproof material that's easy to keep clean, which is why so many people choose it for their kitchens and bathrooms. In the same way, cultured marble countertops — made of fiberglass, crushed limestone, and other materials — are what most people have in their bathrooms, and they stand up to decades of use and wear. Neither surface is indestructible, however. They can both be burned by hot pans and scratched by cutting, so treat with care.

For everyday cleaning, use a sanitizing household cleaner. Most common kitchen stains — mustard, ketchup, coffee, or ink from price stickers — can be rubbed out with a damp sponge sprinkled with baking soda. If the stain persists, make a paste of baking soda and water and a couple of drops of lemon juice. Let dry, and then wipe off with a sponge dipped in clean water.

 Don't clean with abrasive cleaners or steel wool, which can leave scratches that not only make the countertop look unattractive, but also catch dirt and breed germs.

Solid surfaces (Corian)

Nonporous, solid surfaces with names like Corian, Avonite, and Swanstone can withstand a lot of punishment. The beauty of these counters is that they're all one piece, so you don't have seams between the counter and the backsplash or the sink. Often, the sink is made of the same material as the countertop. The down side is that these surfaces tend to scratch from cutting (so use a cutting board, instead), stain if your surface is light in color, and burn (so don't place hot pans directly on the surface).

For daily cleaning, use a two-sided scrubbing pad with a sponge on one side and scouring pad on the other. Wipe up spills with soap and water. Use the scouring pad side with powdered cleanser to get rid of stains, burn marks, or greasy spots.

Granite and engineered stone counters

Granite and engineered stone countertops (those, like Silestone and Ceasarstone, made of a mix of granite and other stones, glued together) are relatively easy to care for, because the surfaces are hard and non-porous. You can place hot pans on the surface without burning, and you can cut directly on the surface. You shouldn't have to seal the material, unless you're told otherwise when the counter is installed.

To clean, avoid harsh chemicals use a mild solution of water and a vegetable-based detergent, such as Murphy's Oil Soap on a soft cloth. You can use a scrubbing pad to get rid of caked on spills, but avoid using steel wool.

Floors

See Chapter 8 for how to clean your specific type of floor. Just be sure to wipe up spills as soon as they occur. And don't be afraid to use your vacuum in the kitchen and bathroom. With the right attachments, vacuuming is faster and removes dirt and hair better than sweeping. Use the crevice tool to reach under the range or sinks, around the baseboards, and behind the refrigerator and toilet.

Sinks and faucets

Use the following tips to keep your sinks shiny and your faucets sparkling:

❃ **Stainless steel sinks:** Clean with a sponge dipped in hot, sudsy water or wipe off with a soft cloth and window cleaner. To polish, rub with a cut lemon or a cloth dampened with lemon juice.

❃ **Porcelain sinks:** Clean regularly with a nonabrasive household cleaner or with baking soda sprinkled on a damp sponge. If your white sink is stained, fill with a solution of 3 tablespoons of bleach per gallon of water. Let sit for an hour, remove, and rinse off.

❃ **Faucets:** Spray glass cleaner on a dry cloth and give the faucets a quick swipe. Or rub with a little baking soda on a slightly damp cloth. Don't use steel wool or any abrasive cleaner — either could scratch the finish. Remove lime deposits caused by hard water by wiping with a white vinegar and water solution.

Cleaning Stoves and Ovens

The key to keeping the stove clean is to wipe up spills as they happen. After all, an appliance that gets hot enough to bake food will logically also turn spilled food and grease spatters into something akin to cement. But a spill that's still hot is usually soft and easily wiped up.

A surefire stain maker is the mixing spoon that you probably lay on the stovetop while we're cooking. If you don't have a spoon rest, lay your spoons on a damp sponge on the cooktop (the cooking surface). After you're finished, just clean off the sponge in sudsy water or throw it in the dishwasher.

Cleaning the cooktop

Stovetops and *backsplashes* (the wall area behind stovetop) are subject to stains from boiled-over pots, spilled gravy, and spattering grease.

For a thorough cleanup of the cooktop, remove the *control knobs* (the knobs that control the level of heat for each burner) and the *grates* (the metal pieces on which you set your pans — you usually find them only on gas cooktops). Soak them in the sink in warm soapsuds. If you have pans (called *drip pans*) under the grates or *coils* (the electric-stove version of grates) and they're removable, put them in the same solution to soak. By the time you get finished cleaning the rest of the stove, the dirt should be falling off the knobs, grates, and drip pans. Rinse them and dry thoroughly before you put them back in place. You don't want any water dripping underneath or behind the inside of the stove.

Coils on electric stoves are basically self-cleaning. Just turn on high to burn off any spill. Because solid heating elements are sealed to the cooktop, spills stay on the surface rather than going into drip pans. To clean, wait until the heating element cools and wipe with hot-sudsy water. Dry off by putting the element on medium setting for a couple of minutes. Be careful with your coils; they can break if you hit them or drop heavy objects on them.

 Never use harsh scrubbing pads or steel wool on any cooktop, no matter how nasty the spill. It can scratch the surface.

Glass cooktops

Although glass surfaces are relatively easy to care for, special attention must be taken because of their sensitivity to dirt. Bottoms of pots and pans should be clean when you place them on a cooktop. Make sure the rag or sponge you use to wipe them off has no dirt or grease on it left over from cleaning the rest of the kitchen. Any residue on the cloth can leave a film on the stove that often doesn't appear until the stove is heated up the next time.

Clean your cooktop when cool with mild dishwashing liquid and water or with a cleaner made especially for this type of cooktop. Rinse well and buff with a dry cloth. Treat a burned-on spill with a baking soda and water paste or a nonabrasive powder. Remove stuck-on food with a nonabrasive scrubber.

Stainless steel stoves

If your stovetop or the front of your oven is made of stainless steel, use caution while cleaning so that you don't scratch the surface. Clean spots with a baking soda and water paste or a solution made specifically for stainless steel. Rinse and wipe with a paper towel. Give it extra shine with a cloth dampened with vinegar. You can also wipe with a cloth slightly dampened with mineral oil, and then rinse and dry with a soft cloth.

Cleaning the oven

Many new ovens (also called *ranges* when the entire unit includes both an oven and a cooktop) have self-cleaning features that do much of the cleaning for you. Lucky you, if you have a new one — they require only minimal care. If you don't fall into this category, you have to use a little more energy and elbow grease to keep yours clean.

 If you notice something dripping while you're baking, sprinkle some salt on it immediately after the oven is turned off but still warm. Then, when the oven is cool, wipe off all the salt and the stain.

The following list discusses some items in every oven that need special attention:

✻ **Oven racks:** First remove the racks and set them to soak in a solution of hot soapy water. Extra greasy racks should be put in a stronger solution of $1/2$ cup ammonia to $1/2$ gallon hot water. After they've soaked, get rid of burned-on dirt with a plastic scrubber. Wear rubber gloves when working with heavy ammonia solutions.

✻ **Glass doors and windows:** Wipe off with a cloth dipped in ammonia. Let the solution soak into the surface and then clean it off with a sponge and hot water. Scrub any remaining spots with a plastic scrubber. Never use a steel wool pad, which will scratch the glass.

Conventional oven

A relatively painless way to clean the oven — and avoid spraying a whole lot of chemicals inside — is to place a cup of ammonia in a cold oven. Shut the door and leave it overnight. When you open the oven door the next day, stand back and turn your face away. The fumes are strong but dissipate rapidly. Pour the ammonia down the sink and flush with plenty of warm water. Wear rubber gloves and wipe off the loosened food and grease with paper towels or an old rag. Rub any stubborn spots with a plastic scrubber and a mixture of liquid dishwashing detergent and soapy water. Rinse the oven, first with a vinegar and water solution and then with clean water.

If you've let the oven go for a long time, the ammonia trick may not be strong enough. You may need to use a commercial oven cleaner. Because commercial oven cleaners are extremely caustic, you should follow the instructions on the can carefully. Never spray oven cleaner in a hot oven. Put strips of aluminum foil over the heating elements, oven wiring, and thermostat to protect them. Put paper on the floor and nearby countertops, put on rubber gloves, and wear an apron or an old shirt. Make sure that you rinse the oven carefully according to the instructions on the can and remove every speck of cleaner before you turn the oven on again.

107

 Also remember that putting ammonia and bleach together is a killer. When the two fumes meet, they create a poison that can kill you in minutes. If you've used ammonia in your oven and are moving on to the commercial cleaner, make sure the cleaner does not contain bleach.

Self-cleaning ovens

This type of oven uses high heat to burn off soil and reduce the grime to a light coating of ash at the bottom. You adjust the oven to the right setting, and it does the dirty work for you. Before you start the cleaning process, give the oven a fast wipe with a damp cloth to get rid of anything that may cause smoke during the cleaning process.

 Never clean the gasket itself; cleaning fluids, even water, can damage it. Always follow the manufacturer's directions for cleaning the oven and never use commercial oven cleaner for this type of surface.

Cleaning the Refrigerator

A thorough, big-time cleaning takes a little work, but you don't have to do it that often. Here's how:

1   **First, turn off the refrigerator.**

    Be sure to clean your refrigerator when it's nearly empty of food; transfer any food you do have to a friend's refrigerator temporarily.

2   **Remove all the shelves and drawers and let them come to room temperature.**

3   **Wash shelves and drawers in warm, sudsy water; rinse off and dry.**

4   **In a small bucket, mix a solution of 2 tablespoons baking soda and 1 quart warm water.**

5   **Dip a sponge in the solution and wash down the walls.**

6   **Rinse with clean water and dry with a soft towel or paper towels.**

7   **Wash the *gasket* (the rubber seal between the door and the refrigerator) with the baking soda solution and use a toothbrush to clean off any dirt in the folds. Rinse and dry.**

To spot-clean, use the same baking soda solution in Step 4 to wipe off any stains or spills.

Cleaning Small Appliances

Most people keep a battery of small appliances on their countertops. They, too, must be cleaned after every use and also have the unfortunate habit of accumulating dirt and grime while just sitting on the countertop. Because most are made of heavy-duty plastic, though, they need only a quick wipe-down when you're cleaning the countertop.

* **Blender:** Cleaning the blender by hand is simple and fun. Just fill it halfway with water and squirt ½ teaspoon liquid dishwashing detergent into it. Put the lid back on and turn the blender on low for about 30 seconds. Rinse and dry. Sponge down the base with a warm sudsy solution or use a spray household cleaner. The narrow areas around the edges of the buttons can be cleaned with a cotton swab dipped in cleaning solution.

* **Food processor:** Many people shy away from using a food processor because it's often easier to wash one knife than all the parts of the processor. For some jobs, however, a food processor is a lifesaver. Cleanup is much easier if you rinse off the blades and bowls as you go. Either wash the components by hand or put them on the top shelf of the dishwasher, depending on the recommendations in your instruction manual.

* **Can opener:** Remove the detachable blade and clean after each use. Wipe the other parts with a sponge dipped in warm, soapy water.

* **Coffeemaker:** The removable parts of a drip coffeemaker — the pot, lid, and basket — can be washed by hand in a sudsy solution or on the top rack of the dishwasher.

  If you detect a bitter taste in your coffee, you know it's time for a thorough internal cleaning. Once a month is usually a good guideline. Pour 4 cups of white distilled vinegar into the coffeepot and add 6 cups of water. Pour this solution into the coffeemaker. Put a filter in the basket and press the *On* button just like you would to make a cup of coffee. (Some coffeemakers have special clean cycles, so check your manual first before cleaning.) When about half of this mixture has dripped into the pot, turn off the machine and let it sit for about 30 minutes. Pour the mixture back into the machine, turn it on and let the full solution run through. Afterward, run a couple of pots of plain water through the machine to rinse out all the vinegar.

* **Toaster (or toaster oven):** Always unplug the toaster before you start cleaning it. Let it cool. Open the crumb tray and empty it or turn the toaster upside down over a trash can and shake it. Clean

out the corners of the toaster's interior and dislodge any remaining crumbs with a soft brush. Wipe the tray with a damp cloth. Dry off thoroughly. If you have a toaster oven, remove the rack and metal tray and soak them in sudsy water or put the rack and tray in the dishwasher according to your instruction manual.

If the outside of your toaster is chrome, spray window cleaner on a damp cloth and wipe. Buff with a dry cloth. Stubborn spots can be treated by wiping with a damp plastic scrubber and baking soda. Plastic exteriors should be wiped down with a sponge dipped in a sudsy solution. Never immerse the toaster in water or drip anything inside.

Doing Dishes without Doing Them In

Doing dishes is one of those inevitable tasks that must be performed day in and day out. But whether you're lucky enough to have an automatic dishwasher or you have to do it by hand, you can definitely make the process easier and more efficient.

Using the automatic dishwasher

When you get your dishwasher, be sure to read the manufacturer's instructions for loading. Every model has different features and is designed differently, so what may work for one model may not be efficient for another.

Here's a list of some general principles recommended by manufacturers on how to get the most from your dishwasher.

* **Scrape off food and lightly rinse the dishes before putting them in.** Many manufacturers claim that you can skip this step, but leaving large pieces of food on dishes only invites problems.

* **Place all the dishes and pans so the soiled areas are facing the center** where the hot water spray comes from.

* **Don't overload the dishwasher.** If dishes are too close together, the water and detergent can't get in between them to clean everything.

* **Wash any plastic, heat-sensitive items on the top rack** as far away from any heat sources as possible.

* **Load unlike pieces of silverware together.** Don't nest all the spoons and forks together in one compartment. They may cradle inside one another and prevent water from hitting all the sides of each piece.

110

☺ ☺ ☹ ☺ ☺ ☹ ☺ ☺ ☹ ☺ ☺ ☹ ☺ ☺ ☹ ☺ ☺ ☺ ☹ ☺

❋ **Put sharp items in the silverware basket with the points down** to prevent any cuts when reaching into the dishwasher.

❋ **Lay long-handled utensils, such as kitchen spatulas, flat in the top rack so they don't fall through to block the wash arms.** Small and lightweight items should also be placed so that they don't fall through the racks.

Washing dishes by hand

While you're cooking, fill the sink with soapy water and put the mixing bowls, measuring spoons, and other utensils in it to soak as you use them. This will loosen most of the grime before you actually get ready to wash. Try to do the dishes right after the meal. If you can't, at least wipe off any food with a scraper, stack the dishes, and soak the pans in hot water.

 Use hot water to soak pans that are greasy or were used to cook sugary foods. Use cold water to soak pans with milk, eggs, or starchy food residue on them. Hot water will set dairy and starchy food residue and make it harder to get off.

Fill up the sink or dishpan with the hottest water your hands can stand. Put a couple of squirts of dishwashing liquid in the pan and swish around the water to create some suds and dissolve the liquid.

The dishwater will stay cleaner longer if you wash the least soiled items first and move on to the more heavily soiled. Follow this order when washing:

❋ Glasses

❋ Silverware

❋ Eating dishes

❋ Serving dishes

❋ Cooking utensils

❋ Pots and pans

Change the water when it becomes dirty or greasy. Rinse the dishes in hot water, either under the faucet or by dipping in a half-full pan of hot water. Change the rinse water as it becomes sudsy.

Keeping Cookware Cooking: Pots, Pans, and Serving Dishes

If you want your pots to last a long time, follow these basic tips to avoid problems:

* **Don't run cold water into a hot pan.** It can cause metal to warp and can even crack glass or earthenware.

* **Don't use excessive heat on pans.** Keep flames on gas stoves low enough so that they touch only the bottom of the pan. Check the care instructions before you put a pan in a hot oven or under the broiler.

* **Always scour pans with plastic scrubbers first.** If a stain won't come off, try soaking the stain off the pan. If you feel you need a metal scraper to get it clean, test it on the side or bottom of the pan first. Metal scrubbers can remove the finish on some cookware.

 Always follow the manufacturer's recommendations for cleaning your cookware. If you no longer have the documentation that came with your cookware, check out the manufacturer's Web site. Just type the brand name of your cookware (such as Revereware, CorningWare, Pyrex, or Calphalon) in your favorite search engine to find cleaning instructions, storage ideas, and cooking tips.

Cleaning aluminum

Aluminum pans are excellent heat conductors, but you must treat them with care to avoid discoloration or staining.

* Don't wash anodized aluminum pans in the dishwasher — washing by hand in hot, sudsy water is best.

* Don't leave water soaking in aluminum utensils or store moist foods in aluminum containers, because chemicals in some foods and water may cause pitting in the metal, odors, and bad flavors.

Remove stains or discoloration in aluminum pots by boiling a solution of 1 to 2 tablespoons cream of tartar or lemon juice to each quart of water for about 10 minutes. To remove burned-on food, boil water in the pan until it loosens the crud. Then scour with a soap-filled steel wool pad, if necessary.

Dealing with non-stick finishes

Remove stubborn stains on non-stick finishes with either one of these two solutions:

✸ 1 cup water, 2 tablespoons baking soda, and 3 tablespoons oxygen bleach

✸ 3 tablespoons automatic dishwasher detergent and 1 cup water

Put the solution in the pan and let it boil on the stove for 15 minutes. Wash the pan, rinse, and dry. Season the pan by wiping the inside lightly with cooking oil before using it again.

 To avoid stains, use medium to low heat for cooking. Extremely high temperatures used continuously discolor the surface.

Mildew Loves Your Bathroom

Keep mildew at bay by reducing the humidity in your bathroom. Your best bet is to install a ceiling fan that's vented to the outside. If you have a window in the bathroom, open it slightly when weather permits. Get the air flowing to dry up the humidity and get rid of mildew spores.

Make a point of drying off anything that you use for bathing as soon as possible. After you get out of the shower, pull back the curtain across the length of the tub so that air can get to the total surface and dry it without leaving any damp spots that breed mildew. If you have a shower enclosure, leave the shower door open slightly after you're finished to give steam a chance to escape.

Don't leave used towels in lumps on the floor. Make a family rule: Everyone hangs up his or her towel. If you don't have enough hanging space, install an over-the-door rack or peg hooks on the wall to hang towels to dry.

Here's a plan of attack for getting rid of mildew in specific areas of your bathroom:

✸ **Tile:** Remove mildew spots from tile by wiping with a solution of ¼ cup bleach to 1 quart water. Before using bleach, make sure that no residue is left on the tile from any cleaning solutions that contain ammonia, because breathing in a combination of bleach and ammonia fumes can kill you. Rinse the surface well after washing.

✿ **Grout:** Clean the grout with a commercial mildew stain remover or wipe with the bleach and water mixture mentioned in the preceding bullet. Apply the solution with a cloth or sponge to avoid splattering the bleach on clothes or nearby fabric.

To get into the hard-to-reach spot between the wall and the tub, soak paper towels or cotton balls in the bleach and water solution and place against the grout. Leave in place for a couple of hours so that the bleach penetrates the grout, and then rinse well. Scrub lightly with a soft toothbrush dipped in the bleach solution, if necessary.

✿ **Shower curtain:** If your shower curtain is mildew-ridden, take it outside and brush off all the dark stuff. Then throw it in the washer in warm water on the delicate cycle. Put in ½ cup detergent and ½ cup baking soda for the wash and 1 cup white vinegar in the rinse cycle to prevent further mildewing. Take the curtain out before the final spin cycle and hang it over a curtain rod to dry. If any mildew still exists, brush it off.

✿ **Walls:** If your walls have just a small amount of mildew, wash them with a relatively mild solution of 1 part bleach to 5 parts water. Rinse well.

If the mildew is running rampant, consider repainting the room. Before you repaint, though, you have to kill off *all* the existing mildew. This takes a strong solution of 1 part bleach to 1 part water or a store-bought mildew-fighting solution. Use the solution all over the ceiling and walls. Wear protective eye covering and long-sleeved clothing and ventilate the area well. After killing the mildew, add a coat of shellac or stain-killing primer to keep the mildew from growing again in the same spots. Look for mildew-resistant paint at your local home center.

Deep Cleaning the Entire Bathroom

About once a week, give your bathroom a really good scrubbing. This section gives you tips on getting the whole room thoroughly clean, with special concentration on the big three: shower, tub, and toilet. These areas are the real victims of soap scum and water deposits, so they take a little more elbow grease than the rest of the bathroom.

Shining shower enclosures

Nothing is worse than stepping into a dirty shower stall. You want to get clean, but you're surrounded by dirt. To deep clean a shower stall that has a heavy layer of soap scum, do the following:

☺ ☺ ☹ ☺ ☺ ☹ ☺ ☺ ☹ ☺ ☺ ☺ ☹ ☺ ☺ ☹ ☺ ☺ ☺ ☹ ☺

1   **Turn on the shower for a few minutes at the hottest tempera-ture to loosen the dirt.**

2   **Turn off the water, ventilate the room, put on rubber gloves, and spray all surfaces with a heavy-duty cleaner or soap scum remover.**

As an alternative, use a mixture of $\frac{1}{2}$ cup vinegar, 1 cup ammonia, and $\frac{1}{4}$ cup baking soda in 1 gallon water. If you've previously used bleach on the walls, don't use any solution containing ammonia for several days.

3   **Let the cleaner soak into the walls for a couple of minutes.**

4   **Use the showerhead to rinse the walls.**

To clean out the shower-door track, squirt it with an all-purpose cleaner, and scrub it with a toothbrush or a rag wound around a screwdriver.

Pour some lemon oil on a rag and rub it into the metal frame and track to remove hard-water stains. Wipe the doors and walls of the shower with a light coating of lemon oil. It discourages future build-up of soap scum and mineral deposits. (Cover the bottom of the stall with a towel while you're applying the oil to prevent the oil from spilling on the floor and making it very slippery.)

Remove tough water spots from the glass door and give it extra sparkle by rubbing it with a mixture of clear vinegar and water. Dry with a soft cloth.

Rub-a-dubbing the tub

Keep a spray bottle in the bath area that's filled with 2 teaspoons liquid dishwashing detergent and 1 teaspoon white vinegar in water. Spray this solution on the walls of the tub, let it sit for a couple of minutes, and then wipe it down.

Even though your tub seems indestructible, it's not. Using harsh abrasives or steel wool can damage the finish.

Cleaning the dreaded toilet

Read the label on any toilet bowl cleaner you buy, because most cleaners are strong stuff. Always wear rubber gloves and be careful not to drip any-thing on the countertops or other surfaces. Spray toilet bowl cleaner into the bowl and under the rim, swish around with a brush, and then flush.

Spray the rim, seat, hinges, bottom, and outside of the tank with all-purpose cleaner. Wipe off with a paper towel and throw the paper away — in the wastebasket, not in the toilet. (Paper towels can clog drains.) Use a toothbrush, if necessary, to get into the crevices around the hinges and bottom of the tank. After cleaning the toilet bowl, rinse and flush away any cleaner before using a cleaner on the outside of the toilet.

 If you use an in-tank cleaner, don't put any other cleaner in the toilet until the in-tank cleaner is all used up and the water is totally clear.

To treat stains the easy way, pour $\frac{1}{2}$ cup bleach into the toilet bowl. Let it soak for a couple of hours, scrub the toilet with a brush, and then flush.

 Be careful not to mix any chemicals (especially bleach and ammonia) or let two chemicals that could cause toxic fumes come into contact with each other.

Cleaning the rest of the room

Finish up the items in this list, and you're done!

- **Towel racks:** Give wood towel racks a nice finish by periodically applying furniture polish with a soft cloth. Rub gently so that the polish can penetrate the wood. Clean chrome towel racks with a light-duty all-purpose cleaner and wipe dry.

- **Mirrors:** Attack any smudges by dampening a paper towel or a wad of toilet paper with rubbing alcohol and wiping the area — no rinsing necessary. This not only leaves the mirror sparkling clean but also removes any sticky residue of hair spray or spots of toothpaste.

- **Soap dishes:** Take out the soap and rinse the dish with water. Keep soap from getting gummy by putting a small piece of nylon mesh (from a fruit or onion bag) under the soap in the dish.

- **Grout:** If your countertop or wall grout is dirty, make a paste of baking soda and water and rub it into the grout with a sponge or toothbrush. Wipe off and rinse thoroughly.

- **Bath rugs:** A cotton or synthetic rug with a woven backing can usually be machine washed and dried on a medium setting. Check the care label to see if it's washable. Wash rugs separately or with towels of a similar color, because these rugs can throw off lots of lint. If your rug has a latex backing, wash in cold water and tumble dry on low.

Chapter 11

Washing Your Clothes in a Snap

The secret to easy-care washing is knowing your fabrics and understanding how to treat them. Each garment or other fabric item has a care label that tells you what the item is made of and how to care for it. These labels give you enormous help in cleaning your clothes. The care label tells you:

✿ Exactly what type of cleaning method works best

✿ What wash-water temperatures to use

✿ How to dry and iron the item

✿ How *not* to treat the item

✿ What the fiber content is, which helps you determine how delicate the item is and how to treat a stain

If your label is missing but you know what the fabric is made of, use Table 11-1.

☺ ☺ ☹ ☺ ☺ ☹ ☺ ☺ ☹ ☺ ☺ ☹ ☺ ☺ ☹ ☺ ☺ ☺ ☺ ☹ ☺

Table 11-1 Fabric Care

Fabric	How to Clean It	How to Dry It	Special Care
Acrylic	Machine wash or hand wash in warm water according to label.	Dry on low or air fluff setting.	Turn garment inside out to avoid pilling. For sweaters, pull into shape after washing and dry flat on a towel.
Cotton	Wash in gentle cycle or by hand according to care label. Use warm water for *colorfast* fabrics (those that don't run or bleed); use cold water for bright colors that bleed.	Line dry or machine dry on low setting. Remove from dryer while damp. Remove cotton knits while damp and pull into shape. Dry flat on a towel.	Iron while damp on hot set.
Denim	Can be cotton or cotton blend. Machine wash inside out in water. Wash separately until color no longer bleeds.	Dry on low to avoid shrinkage.	Iron damp with hot iron.
Linen	Dry clean to keep finish crisp. Wash in gentle cycle in cold or warm water. Check for colorfastness.	Line or machine dry on low setting. Remove from dryer while damp.	Iron on wrong side; use hot iron on heavy linens; iron set on low for blends and lightweights.
Nylon	Hand or machine wash on gentle cycle in warm water. Use all-purpose detergent.	Drip dry or machine dry on permanent press cycle.	If necessary, iron on cool setting.
Polyester	Machine wash on warm setting with all-purpose detergent.	Drip dry or machine dry on low setting. Turn inside out to avoid pilling.	Don't wash with greasy items. Iron on warm setting.
Rayon	May also be called viscose. Dry clean to retain body. If you do have a label it says "washable," hand wash or machine wash in warm water with a mild detergent.	Machine dry on low setting. Remove while damp and pull into shape.	Don't twist or wring. Iron damp on warm setting.

☺ ☺ ☹ ☺ ☺ ☹ ☺ ☺ ☹ ☺ ☺ ☹ ☺ ☺ ☹ ☺ ☺ ☺ ☹ ☺ ☺

Fabric	How to Clean It	How to Dry It	Special Care
Silk	Dry clean heavier weight or colored silk. If you do have a label and it says "washable," hand wash in cold water with mild or cold-water detergent. Rinse well. Test for colorfastness first (see the "Pretreating Stains" section for details.)	Roll in towel to blot dry; then air dry.	Iron damp on cool setting. Don't bleach.
Spandex	Hand or machine wash in lukewarm water in gentle cycle.	Line dry or machine on low temperature.	Don't use bleach. Avoid overdrying.

Many garments today are a combination of fibers that can sometimes throw you for a loop when you're trying to figure out how to treat them. A general rule is to clean items as though they were made only of the highest percentage fiber. For example, if a garment is 90 percent linen and 10 percent rayon, clean it like a linen garment. But when you treat a stain, start with a stain-removal product safe for the most delicate fiber (in this case, the rayon) in the blend.

Choosing Laundry Products

You can choose from a number of products to get your clothes clean. All you have to do is walk down the laundry aisle in a grocery store, and you're inundated by boxes and jugs that promise lots of things. What's in these containers, and which ones should you use for what?

✺ Heavy-duty detergents are available in liquid or granular form for just about all washables, including heavily soiled items. They contain ingredients that help break down grease and oil and inactivate water hardness. Use the liquid form if you like to pretreat oily or greasy spots with detergent.

✺ Light-duty detergents in liquid or powder form are good for delicate washable fabrics, baby clothes, and lightly soiled items.

✺ Ultra detergents are more concentrated and come in liquid or granular form. The boxes are smaller, and you use a smaller amount for each normal load — a great bonus if you live in an apartment and have limited storage space.

Whiten and brighten: Chlorine or oxygen bleach

If you have time to lay your clothes out in the sunlight to whiten, you may want to forgo bleach. But most people need some extra help to keep clothes white and bright, and that means bleach. Bleach whitens and gets rid of stains when used in conjunction with a detergent. The two most common man-made bleaches are chlorine bleach and oxygen bleach.

Remember, bleaches are strong stuff and, if used incorrectly, can permanently damage fabric. Never mix bleaches with other household chemicals or cleaning supplies, especially ammonia, rust removers, vinegars, and toilet bowl cleaners. The mixture can produce noxious fumes that can kill you.

Using chlorine bleach

Chlorine has always been the powerhouse bleach, and it's more effective than oxygen bleach on cottons, linens, and most synthetics. But it's also the most hazardous, and chlorine bleach can ruin some fabrics. Here are some tips to keep in mind when working with chlorine bleach:

* **Never pour bleach directly on fabric.** Always dilute it according to the instructions on the label. Used full strength, bleach can cause permanent spotting and dissolve the fabric.

* **Be careful with the bleach bottle.** If you accidentally spill it on rugs, furniture, or clothing, there's a good chance that the stain will be permanent.

* **Be cautious of the amount you put in the wash.** Too much bleach can cause yellowing or weakening of the fibers in the cloth. Always check the manufacturer's recommendations for the proper amount.

* **Bleach on a schedule.** Bleaching too frequently can harm your clothes. Be conservative and use bleach every second or third load.

* **Don't add chlorine bleach at the beginning of the wash cycle.** Put it in the machine about five minutes after the cycle has begun. This gives the machine plenty of time to fill up with water and thoroughly moisten all the clothes. To be extra safe, dilute the bleach in 1 quart water first.

* **Use chlorine bleach only on washable whites and colorfast fabrics.** Always check the label first.

If you're in doubt about colorfastness, try this simple test to see whether the fabric is bleach-safe:

1   Mix together 1 tablespoon of chlorine bleach and ¹/₄ cup of water.

2   Dip a cotton swab in this solution and put a drop on a hidden area, such as a seam. Leave it on for 1 minute.

3   Blot with a paper towel and check for color change.

If there's no color change, you can safely bleach the article. If the garment has any decorative trim, be sure to check that, too. Rinse your test fabric thoroughly.

Using all-fabric oxygen bleach

Less harsh than chlorine bleach, oxygen bleach comes in dry and liquid forms and can be used on most washable fabrics, including colored fabrics, washable silks and wools, and bleachable whites. It has a more gentle bleaching action to whiten whites that aren't safe for chlorine bleach.

 If the care label on a fabric says "Do not bleach," don't use any bleach, not even oxygen bleach.

Other useful laundry aids

If only stains never mysteriously appeared on your clothes, and clothes always came out of the dryer soft and wrinkle-free. Alas, stains happen and stiff, wrinkly clothes do happen, so here are a few other laundry aids to keep your clothes looking bright and feeling soft.

✿   **Enzyme presoaks** (like Biz, Clorox 2, or Spray 'N' Wash Pink Liquid) are used to soak stains prior to washing and also to boost the cleaning power of detergents. They're especially effective on blood, protein, or food stains such as egg, milk, coffee, and baby food. They can also work on things like grass stains and fruit juice.

✿   **Prewash stain removers** come in several different forms — spray, liquids, sticks, and aerosols are used to treat heavily soiled areas, like collars and cuffs, or to treat spots and stains prior to washing.

- **Fabric softeners** reduce static cling (the stuff that makes your clothing stick to arms, legs, slips, hose, and other things), especially on nylon, polyester, and acrylic fabric. They also make fabrics feel soft and fluffy. Another bonus: Fabric softeners reduce wrinkling and thus cut ironing time (see Chapter 12).

- **Dryer sheets** can be more convenient than fabric softeners because you can just throw them into the dryer. As the dryer heats up, the chemicals in the sheets transfer to the clothes, reducing static cling. They aren't quite as effective in penetrating all the clothes as the liquid form is, and they usually don't make clothes softer.

Sorting and Checking Your Clothes

When sorting your laundry, match likes with likes — separating dark colors from light, sturdy fabrics from delicate ones, and so on. When you sort your clothes well, you end up with a machine-load of items that require the same treatment. Sorting properly can reduce a lot of laundry problems.

Hand washing your clothes

If you find a label that says "hand wash" or you'd just feel better hand washing an item, follow these steps:

1 Put your detergent or soap in a basin with either warm or cold water, depending on the care label instructions and the delicacy of the fabric.

2 Swish the garment gently through the suds a few times, but don't wring or twist it.

3 Soak the item for about 5 minutes.

   If not colorfast and the garment is bleeding dye, soak it for only 2 minutes.

4 Gently squeeze out the detergent.

5 Empty the basin and refill it with clean, cold water.

6 Rinse the garment thoroughly in clean, cold water until you've removed all the soap.

   Keep rinsing until the water doesn't feel slippery and no suds appear when you push water through the clothes. Sometimes, you need to rinse two or three times.

7 Lay the item flat on a towel and roll the garment up to absorb moisture.

8 Unroll the garment and hang it on a plastic hanger to dry or lay it flat on a drying frame or towel.

You can sort your clothes in many different ways; use what works best for you. The following section provides some tips to help you sort:

🌸 Separate white and light-colored clothes from dark ones. Even small amounts of dye in water can transfer to light-colored fabrics and ruin them.

🌸 Separate any delicate fabrics, sheers, or items requiring a delicate cycle and low water temperature from sturdy ones.

🌸 Separate items that produce a lot of lint (chenille robes, towels, and sweat suits, to name a few) from items that attract and show lint (dark fabrics, synthetics, and permanent press).

🌸 Separate heavily soiled items, such as work clothes or items with grease stains, from lightly soiled items. Otherwise, light colors may pick up some of the soil and get a gray tinge to them.

🌸 Separate any items marked "hand wash" or "dry clean only." To hand wash, read the "Hand washing your clothes" sidebar in this chapter. Take dry-clean-only products to your local drycleaner.

🌸 Separate any items that are marked "wash separately," which means that the color will run for the first few washings. To see whether the color is still bleeding, look at the suds in the wash water or wash the item with a small piece of white cloth to see whether the cloth absorbs any color.

 Always empty pockets while sorting the laundry. Pens, markers, crayons, and sharp items can damage your clothes and your washer or dryer if run through a single cycle.

Pretreating Stains

Pretreat dirty cuffs, collars, and any noticeable soil by rubbing on liquid detergent, prewash stain remover, or a paste of powdered detergent and water.

Here are some guidelines for smart stain removal:

🌸 **Treat the stain as soon as you can.** Many spots and spills are just laying on the surface of the fabric when they first happen and will be no problem if removed immediately. If they dry or sit for a few days, they'll be absorbed into the fibers, and your chance of removing them gets dimmer and dimmer.

🌸 **Remove as much of the spill as you can before applying any stain-removing product.** If you have a mound of pudding, a blob of catsup, or a plop of tuna salad, use a dull knife or spoon to lift off the food or other product.

☺ ☺ ☺ ☺ ☺ ☺ ☺ ☺ ☺ ☺ ☺ ☺ ☺ ☺ ☺ ☺ ☺ ☺ ☺

❀ **Always read the care label of the garment before you apply any stain remover.** Different fabrics require different stain removers. And some fabrics can be damaged by something as innocuous as water.

❀ **Try to identify what the stain is before you start working on it.** Some stains can be permanently set if you use the wrong treatment. If you're in doubt, rinse or soak the fabric in cold water before laundering. Check out the following section for tips on dealing with specific stains.

❀ **Always pretest the stain remover for colorfastness before you apply it to the whole garment.** Put a drop of it on a seam or on the underside of the cuff. Rinse and let dry. If no color loss or fabric damage occurs, proceed with the treatment.

❀ **Blot, don't scrub.** Scrubbing can force the stain into the material and spread it to other parts of the garment. Even worse, it can damage delicate or stretchy fabrics.

❀ **Be careful not to spread the stain while you're treating it.** Center the side of the fabric with the stain over an absorbent cloth like a diaper or an old, clean, white towel. Keep turning the cloth or towel over to absorb the liquid as you apply the stain-removing liquid. This makes sure that the stain is driven into the towel and not farther into the fabric.

❀ **Be patient.** Sometimes you may have to apply a treatment two or three times before the stain comes off.

Always rinse or launder washable items to remove the residue left from the stain and the stain remover. Then air dry the garment to make sure the stain is really gone. Some spots are hard to see when the fabric is wet. If you put them in a hot dryer, the stain can be set by the heat, making it impossible to remove.

Removing stains from washable fabrics

Table 11-2 gives you tips for removing stains from washable fabrics.

 Always check the care label to see how to properly clean a garment. If the fabric says to dry clean, let the dry cleaner remove spots with dry-cleaning fluid. If the garment is valuable or you have any doubt about how to clean it, be safe and take it to a dry cleaner.

Table 11-2 Removing Stains from Washable Fabrics

Stain	How to Remove
Blood	Soak fresh stains in cold water. (Don't use hot; it can set the stain.) Saturate the stain with detergent or rub with a laundry pretreat. Wash as usual. Dried stains: Soak in a solution of 1 quart warm water, $\frac{1}{2}$ teaspoon detergent, and 1 tablespoon ammonia for cotton, polyester, rayon, and linen fabrics. Or soak in warm water with enzyme presoak or detergent. If the stain remains, rewash using bleach that's safe for the fabric.
Candlewax	Harden with ice and scrape off with a dull knife. Put the stained area between several clean paper towels and place a sheet of brown paper bag over the towel. Press with a warm iron. Replace paper towels as often as necessary to keep absorbing as much wax as possible. If any marks or stain remain, treat by placing the stain face down on clean towels and sponging with dry-cleaning fluid. Blot dry and then launder as usual. If the stain remains, rewash using a bleach that's safe for the fabric.
Chewing gum	Apply ice to the gum to harden. Scrape off the frozen residue with a dull knife. Sponge with dry cleaning solvent. Rinse and launder.
Chocolate	Rinse the stain with cool water, and then soak in enzyme presoak solution for 30 minutes. Apply detergent to the stain. Wash. If the stain remains, sponge with dry cleaning fluid, rinse, and launder. Or soak in enzyme presoak overnight and launder in the hottest water safe for fabric. Sponge washable wool with mild soapy warm water.
Coffee	First, sponge the stain with cool water to remove as much stain as possible. If safe for fabric, soak in all fabric bleach and warm water. Launder in warm water. If the stain contained cream, soak the stain in cool water and then sponge with dry cleaning fluid. Rinse in cool water and then launder as usual.
Cosmetics	Apply prewash stain remover, liquid detergent, or a paste of detergent and water until the stain is gone. Wash. If the stain remains, use enzyme detergent.
Crayon	Put the stained spot face down on a few folded towels and spraying with WD 40; let stand for several minutes. Turn the fabric over and spray the other side. Apply liquid dishwashing detergent to the stain. Keep replacing towels as they absorb the stain. Wash in hot water with detergent and chlorine or all fabric bleach (if bleach is safe for the fabric) on the longest wash cycle of the machine. Rinse in warm water.

continued

Table 11-2 Removing Stains from Washable Fabrics *(continued)*

Stain	How to Remove
Fruit juice/berries	Soak in cool water for 30 minutes. If safe for the fabric, wash with chlorine bleach. Or soak the fabric in a mixture of 1 table-spoon hydrogen peroxide and 1 quart water. (Test for color-fastness first.) Rinse and launder. Colored fabrics may be treated with oxygen bleach if it's safe for the fabric.
Grass	Rub enzyme presoak or detergent on the stain. Launder in the hottest water possible with bleach that's safe for the fabric.
Grease	Blot the residue or remove with a dull knife. Place the fabric face down on paper towels. Sponge dry-cleaning solvent on the back of the stain until it disappears. Change the paper towels as they absorb the stain. After the cleaning solvent is dry, rinse the garment and then pretreat with detergent or prewash stain remover. Launder in the hottest water that is safe for the fabric.
Ink	Identify exactly what kind of ink you're dealing with: A good bet is to call the company listed on the label and ask them their suggestions about stain removal. If there's no label, pro-ceed cautiously. Some inks may be impossible to remove.
	For ballpoint pen stains, dampen the area around the stain with denatured alcohol. (Look for denatured alcohol near the paint thinner in your home improvement store.) Place the stain face down on some paper towels and apply denatured alcohol or dry-cleaning fluid to the back of the stain. Replace the towels as they absorb the stain. Repeat if the stain remains. Rinse and then launder.
	For other inks, such as felt tip pens or liquid ink, first see whether the stain will wash out by marking a similar piece of fabric with the ink and trying one of these methods:
	Pretreat with prewash stain remover and then launder.
	First flush the stain with cold water. Soak in warm sudsy water with 1 to 4 tablespoons of household ammonia per quart of water. Rinse and then wash using bleach safe for the fabric or hydrogen peroxide and a few drops of water.
	Rub liquid household cleaner into the stain. Rinse. Repeat as many times as needed to remove the stain. Or try the ball-point stain treatment just listed.

☺ ☺ ☹ ☺ ☺ ☹ ☺ ☺ ☹ ☺ ☺ ☹ ☺ ☺ ☹ ☺ ☺ ☺ ☹ ☺

Stain	How to Remove
Mud	Let the stain dry; then brush off as much as you can. Then, soak in cool water. If it's a light stain, apply liquid detergent or a paste of detergent and water; if it's heavy, pretreat with enzyme detergent. Launder. Use bleach that's safe for the fabric if the stain persists.
Mustard	Scrape off as much as possible without spreading the stain. Saturate liquid detergent or prewash enzyme presoak into the stain. Wash in fabric-safe bleach. For nonbleachable fabric, use hydrogen peroxide. Never use ammonia.
Perspiration	Rub with prewash stain remover and then launder in detergent and warm water. If the stain has changed the color of the fabric, sponge with ammonia for fresh stains, vinegar for old stains. (Pretest first.) Rinse with water and then launder. If the stain remains, wash with oxygen (*never* chlorine) bleach.
Shoe polish	Use a spoon to scrape off any residue from the garment. Rinse the stain with dry cleaning fluid or sponge on prewash stain remover. Rinse thoroughly, and then massage detergent into the dampened area. Wash using a bleach safe for the fabric.
Tomato sauce	Rinse in cool water. Soak in prewash stain remover for about 30 minutes. Launder. If the stain persists, soak in equal parts vinegar and water or sponge with a solution of 2 tablespoons ammonia to 1 cup water. Rinse and then launder. Use a bleach safe for the fabric if the stain remains, but *never* mix ammonia and bleach during the same treatment or wash!
Urine	Blot the stain. Soak for a half an hour in enzyme presoak and liquid detergent solution. Rinse in cold water. Sponge any remaining stain with white vinegar. Rinse and wash in warm water. If odor persists, pet stores sell an enzyme product that decreases the smell.
Vomit	Sponge with water and a few drops of ammonia. Then soak in enzyme detergent and water (no bleach). Rinse and then wash.
Wine, red	Cover with table salt and massage gently into the spill. (If white wine is available, you can flush the stain with that.) Rinse in cool water for 15 minutes and then rub the area with prewash stain remover or liquid laundry detergent. Let sit for 15 minutes. Rinse and then launder using a bleach safe for the fabric. Oxygen activated cleaners work well with this stain. If the stain remains, rub with enzyme laundry detergent; then wash with bleach safe for the fabric. The dried stain may not come out, but you can try soaking in ammonia and water or white vinegar.

Getting rid of unknown stains

Often, you don't know exactly what caused the stain; you just know it's there, an annoying reminder of a spill or drip. Although removing these stains is a challenge, it's often worth the time it takes to rescue a garment or other household item. Try to identify the cause of the stain, either greasy or nongreasy:

❀ **Greasy:** You can usually treat grease stains in washable garments with a liquid or spray laundry pretreating product or dry-cleaning fluid.

❀ **Nongreasy:** For nongreasy stains, you can usually sponge or soak them out with water, liquid laundry detergent, and bleach.

If you can't remember whether it was the cheeseburger or the raspberry freeze that you dropped on your shirt, try this method:

1 **Soak the stain in cold water for 20 minutes.**

2 **Apply detergent to the stain.**

Let sit for 30 minutes.

3 **Rinse, and then wash in warm water and air dry.**

4 **If the stain persists, soak in enzyme detergent or presoak overnight and then wash in the hottest water that is safe for the fabric.**

If that doesn't work, wash with a bleach that's safe for the fabric.

Stain still there? Now get really serious by sponging it with dry-cleaning solvent and then applying liquid laundry detergent. Rinse and air dry.

If you think stain is rust, apply a commercial rust remover. Also, remember that you can always try taking the garment to a dry cleaner.

Presoaking Clothes

If clothes are heavily soiled, soak them in a presoak solution or a detergent solution. Sort the clothes according to color before soaking. Then follow these steps:

1 **Mix the detergent or presoak with water in a sink or in a top-loading washer with a presoak cycle.**

Another general-purpose presoak is an oxygen-powered bleach (you'll see the word "oxygen" on the label) mixed with warm water.

☺ ☺ ☹ ☺ ☺ ☹ ☺ ☺ ☹ ☺ ☺ ☹ ☺ ☺ ☹ ☺ ☺ ☹ ☺

2 **Follow the manufacturer's instructions for the length of time that you should soak an item — usually about 30 minutes.**

3 **Spin or wring out garments before starting to wash.**

You may want to do this religiously with kids' clothes, especially play clothes. Let the clothes soak overnight to get the deep down dirt.

And Now, You Wash

You may not like to read instruction manuals, but your washing will be more effective if you're familiar with the manufacturer's instructions of your particular washer and the detergent you're using. Some, like front-loading washers, have quirks that can affect the way you wash your clothes. For most machines, however, you can use the information provided in the sections that follow.

For a top-loading washer, measure the proper amount of detergent and turn on the machine for a few minutes to let some water run into it. Then add the detergent and any other additives you're putting in. Swish it around to dissolve it evenly throughout the water. Then add the clothes. Loading the washer this way is ideal because it allows the detergent to move evenly through the wash. Also keep the following tips in mind:

✽ **Don't overload the washer.** Lay garments in lightly to the top but not past the agitator.

✽ **Avoid wrapping large items like sheets or towels around the agitator.** Instead, put them on one side of the tub. If they become tangled, they won't wash properly and can also put stress on the gears of the machine.

✽ **When you go to put stuff in the wash, separate the heavy items from lightweight ones.** You want a balance of weights, but not all one thing or the other.

Always check the care labels for water temperature and other washing recommendations they provide the only safe way(s) to clean the particular item (or refer to Table 11-1). The following are general guidelines for which water temperature to use when in doubt:

✽ **Hot water:** For heavily soiled items, white and colorfast clothes

✽ **Warm water:** Moderately soiled items, permanent press and wash and wear, washable knits and woolens, and noncolorfast items

✽ **Cold:** Lightly soiled clothes, dark or bright colors that can bleed, delicate or fragile fabrics, and items that might have a tendency to shrink

☺ ☺ ☹ ☺ ☺ ☹ ☺ ☺ ☹ ☺ ☺ ☹ ☺ ☺ ☹ ☺ ☺ ☺ ☺ ☹ ☺

Chapter 12

Drying and Ironing for a Crisp Finish

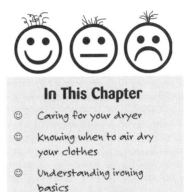

Drying and ironing are the finishing touches of your clothing care. If you do these two tasks correctly, you can reduce your workload and make your clothes look their best. But if you do them incorrectly, you shrink your clothes, ruin the fabrics, and iron in wrinkles instead of ironing them out. If you put some special care into both chores, you can reduce the time you spend in the laundry room.

Dryer Basics

Most dryers are relatively simple to operate. But a few precautions help you have trouble-free operations. As with other appliances, make sure that you read the owner's manual and store it near the dryer, so that you can find it when you have any trouble.

The following hints help you make the most of your dryer time:

❁ **Clean the lint screen.** Before you start any load, clean the lint screen. The dryer is one of the biggest energy hogs in the home, and it runs at half its normal efficiency if the lint screen is clogged, costing you both time and money. In addition, a blocked lint screen can lead to overheating and, possibly, a fire.

❁ **Get rid of sharp objects.** Check clothes before you place them in the dryer. Avoid putting anything sharp or pointed inside. Also close and latch all zippers, clasps, and hooks. Just to be safe, turn anything inside out that could scratch the interior of the dryer.

☺ ☺ ☹ ☺ ☺ ☹ ☺ ☺ ☹ ☺ ☺ ☹ ☺ ☺ ☹ ☺ ☺ ☺ ☹ ☺

❈ **Keep the drum spotless.** Look inside periodically to make sure the drum is clean. Dyes from noncolorfast clothing can leave stains inside the dryer. To clean the dye off, spray some liquid household cleaner into a cloth and rub the stain with it. Let the cleaner sit for a minute or two, and then wipe off the residue with a damp cloth. Put a few rags into the dryer and run it on air-only for about 15 or 20 minutes to eliminate any cleaner residue and make sure the stain is gone.

❈ **Inspect the vents.** A few times a year, check to make sure the dryer is venting properly both inside and outside your home. An obstruction in the *duct* (expanding coil-like tube) or an extra-long duct (more than 50 feet) can restrict the flow of air and cause longer drying times. Look at the exhaust duct outside your house (where air from the dryer flows out) and remove any leaves, branches, or other debris. Inside, take the duct off the vent that links it to the outside and clean it out with a soft brush or the crevice tool of your vacuum cleaner.

Cleaning the vents is important not only for dryer efficiency but also for safety. Lint built up in the duct can start a fire.

❈ **Check the door seal.** If you suspect that your dryer isn't as hot as it should be, check to see whether it is losing heat. Hold a piece of tissue paper in front of the door's edge while the dryer is on. If the paper is drawn toward the door, the seal isn't tight enough and needs to be replaced.

Drying dangers

Some things are downright dangerous to put in the dryer. The following items are better off being dried on the clothesline:

❈ If clothing or rags have been saturated with or come in contact with oil-based paint, paint thinner, oil, gasoline, flammable liquids or solids, or dry cleaning solvent, keep them out of the dryer. These can be extremely flammable when exposed to heat. Wash these items by hand and dry them on a clothesline or *drying rack* (a metal or wooden indoor stand on which you hang clothes), instead.

❈ Never put rubber-coated items, laminated fabrics, vinyl, plastics, foam rubber, or garments that have a trim made from these items on a hot setting in the dryer. They can melt or ignite when exposed to high heat.

❈ Don't put fiberglass curtains or draperies in the dryer unless the label states that the item is machine washable and dryable. You'll embed glass fibers in the dryer that are virtually impossible to remove.

132

Drying how-to's

If you follow these few simple guidelines, you won't have any surprises when you take clothes out of the dryer.

❀ **Always check the care label on clothes,** and check the recommendations in your dryer's owner's manual for fabrics before you put clothes in the dryer. Some delicate clothes can be ruined if you dry them on the wrong setting.

❀ **Turn dark items inside out to cut down on lint accumulation.** Avoid putting them in the dryer with items like light-colored towels or bath mats that usually shed like crazy. If you're drying large items like blankets, put a length of mosquito netting inside to catch the lint.

❀ **Don't put anything in the dryer that still has a stain on it.** If a stain doesn't come out in the wash, re-treat the stain and put the item back in the washer. If you dry it, the stain is set in by the dryer's heat, and chances of it ever coming out are slim.

❀ **Don't put heavy, hard-to-dry items in the same load with lightweight clothes.** Because drying times are different, the lightweight items will be dried properly but the heavier ones will still be damp.

❀ **Don't overload the dryer.** Fill it no more than about half full to leave room for clothes to tumble freely. Put only one washer load in the dryer at a time. This cuts down on wrinkling and on the amount of time needed for clothes to dry.

❀ **Remove clothes from the dryer as soon as the cycle is finished.** When you leave clothes in a pile in the dryer, their accumulated weight causes excessive wrinkling. Take them out and fold them or hang them up immediately after the cycle is finished.

If you're not around to immediately remove the clothes from the dryer, don't despair. Just toss in a wet towel and reset the dryer. Check after 15 or 20 minutes to see whether the wrinkles are gone.

❀ **Shake out each garment when you move it from the washer to the dryer.** Often, items like sheets and pants get tangled around each other. If you don't separate them before putting them in the dryer, all the surfaces won't be exposed evenly to heat.

Drying au natural

There was a day when every backyard had a line full of clothes gently drying in the breeze. Many people believe that air-dried clothes have a sweet smell and soft feel that can't be matched in the dryer. Today, most people opt for the convenience of the dryer, but certain situations dictate when air drying is the best choice. Always check the fabric label for care instructions, and if you have the slightest doubt about putting something in the dryer, hang it on a clothesline. Delicate lingerie, linen fabrics, some cottons, and large items that are too bulky for the dryer are usually good choices for air drying.

For many people, drying outside isn't a workable option. Hanging a clothesline from the 10th floor of an apartment building, for example, is impossible. So, opt for an indoor drying rack or hanging clothes to dry on a hanger (usually hung in your bathroom or other surface that won't be damaged by dripping water).

When you air dry on hangers, use padded hangers so that clothes don't get bumps in them. You don't have padded hangers, you say? Loop some old shoulder pads or pieces of foam rubber over the ends of a hanger and secure with rubber bands.

Some items need to be dried on a flat surface to make sure that they don't get stretched out while drying. Roll up sweaters, knits, and other stretchy fabrics in towels to absorb the excess water. Then unroll each item carefully, reshape it, and lay it flat on a clean, fluffy towel or on a plastic-coated wire rack that fits over the tub. When one side is dry, turn the item over and dry the other.

Using fabric softeners

You can choose from two basic kinds of fabric softeners. According to the Soap and Detergent Association, your particular clothing needs should determine which type you use.

- If you're plagued by static cling (usually associated with synthetic clothing), use dryer sheets. They work in the dryer, where the whole static cling problem starts.
- If you just need a general softening of your clothes, liquid fabric softener added to the rinse water in the machine is better.

Liquid softeners rinse through and permeate the entire load of wash. Dryer sheets affect only the areas that the sheet touches when it's tossed around.

Ironing Basics

If you don't like to iron, you're not alone. But if you take care of your iron and follow a few basic guidelines, you won't cringe at the thought of ironing. Ironing may just go a little easier, and your clothes will look much better.

Taking care of your iron

Although most people take a household iron for granted, it does need proper care and will last for years if given some attention. (And with the price of irons these days, getting as much use out of it as possible is a smart idea!)

 Read the instruction booklet that comes with your iron and follow the directions for cleaning and maintaining it. Check regularly to make sure that the soleplate (the surface of the iron that touches your clothes as you iron) hasn't picked up any dirt. The last thing you want is to iron a new shirt only to find that your iron has deposited a new stain on the front.

Clean your iron only when it is cold *and* unplugged. If your iron has a non-stick soleplate, give it a quick wipe with a damp cloth every now and then. Metal soleplates should be cleaned with a mild detergent and water solution and wiped clean with a soft cloth. Never dip an iron into any cleaning solution. Always put the solution on a cloth and wipe the surface. Avoid the use of abrasive cleaners or scouring pads on either kind of iron — they can scratch the surface.

 Sometimes, the use of spray starch (sprayed on shirts while ironing to make them crisp) leaves a sticky brown residue on the soleplate. To clean it off, mix baking soda and water into a paste, dip a damp cloth into it, and rub it gently on the surface. Clean it off with a dry cloth. Flush out any remaining solution by turning on the iron and pressing the steam control button. Hold the iron over a cloth that can absorb any residue that drips out.

After you've finished ironing, empty the water in the iron and store it in an upright position. If you store the iron flat (the way you iron), excess moisture can drip out of the steam holes.

Ironing how-to's

The proper way to iron is to move the iron back and forth over the length of the fabric. Don't iron in a circular motion. Go with the weave rather than against it to prevent stretching, especially on knit or synthetic fabrics.

Hot stuff: Better safe than sorry

Because an iron is an appliance that heats up, it creates the potential for some accidents around the home. Make sure that you turn the iron controls to "off" when you stop using it, even if just for a minute or two, and leave the iron upright. When you're done ironing, always unplug the iron, even if it has an automatic shut-off.

The water inside the steam tank stays hot for quite a while after the iron is turned off. If the iron tips over or if you tilt it while moving it, watch out for the remaining water in the reservoir, which can cause a burn if spilled on your skin.

Set up the ironing board near a socket so that the cord isn't stretched too far. You don't want anyone to trip over the cord and knock over the iron and the ironing board. Make sure to buy an ironing board that's sturdy on its feet and stands flat on the floor.

Sequencing your ironing: Start low and aim high

If you're ironing several items at once, start by working on the items that need the lowest setting on the iron (usually anything synthetic or silk) and work your way up to the high-setting items (cotton and linen). Because an iron heats up faster than it cools down, you save time by ironing similar items together, rather than waiting for the iron to switch temperatures up and down. A risk in not properly sequencing your ironing is that you may put a hot iron down on something that needs a cool iron and scorch the fabric.

 An iron shouldn't sizzle when it touches fabric. If the iron sizzles, the temperature is too hot.

Preventing shine

Dark fabrics, satin, silk, wool, linen, and crepe fabrics should be ironed on the wrong side of the fabric to prevent shine.

If you already have some shiny patches caused by ironing, place a damp pressing cloth on top of the shiny surface and press. Repeat until the area is dry. Raise the nap of the fabric by gently moving a very soft brush (such as a baby's hairbrush) across the fabric.

Starting with damp clothes

Even if your iron has the greatest steam in the world, clothes just seem to come out much crisper if they're damp when you start to iron. If you're going to iron right after you do the laundry, remove clothes from the dryer while they're a little damp. Another alternative is to keep a spray bottle on the ironing board to give clothes a quick spritz of water before you start. Then roll the clothes up for a couple of minutes to let the water soak in evenly.

 Spray starch also gives clothes a nice finish, but it has a tendency to build up on the soleplate of the iron. To prevent this, spray the starch on the wrong side of the fabric and roll the clothes in a tubular shape to let it soak into the fabric.

Ironing a shirt or blouse

If you iron in the correct order, you're less likely to get wrinkles while you're ironing. Follow these steps for the best results when ironing a shirt or blouse. Figure 12-1 illustrates this process.

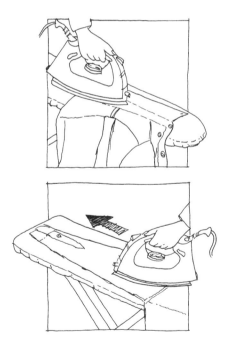

Figure 12-1: Ironing shirts and blouses.

1   Lay the shirt flat on the board and iron the underside of the collar first, working from the ends towards the center.

2   Iron the front side of the collar.

3   Iron the inside of the cuffs, flip them over, and iron the outside.

4   Slip the shoulder over the narrow edge of the board and iron towards the center; repeat on the other side.

5   Press the sleeves, working down from the top near the seam.

6   Iron the body of the shirt, starting on one side and continuing around to the other.

After you finish the body of the shirt, go back and press the collar and any spots that you may have missed or that have become wrinkled.

To prevent wrinkling parts you've already ironed, move the garment away from you across the ironing board as you proceed.

Ironing pants

Follow these instructions to get a good crease on your pants. If your pants have cuffs, iron those first.

1   If necessary, iron the insides of the pockets so that they lay flat.

2   Slip the waistband around the narrow part of the board and iron the top of the pants.

3   Lay the pants flat on the ironing board with the legs on top of each other, match up the inseams and flatten the sides of the legs together.

4   Fold back the leg on top and iron the one on the bottom; flip the pants over and repeat the process.

5   Put the legs together again, match up the inseams, and iron the outside of each leg, making a crease with the steam iron.

Handling buttons, pleats, and other problem areas

Poufs, pleats, buttons, and bows can cause problems while you're ironing. Conquer them all with these tips:

❀   **Delicate buttons** need to be covered to avoid nicking or scratching. Most irons have a built in button groove or channel just above the soleplate. This allows you to press around the button while it rides into the channel.

138

☺ ☺ ☹ ☺ ☺ ☹ ☺ ☺ ☹ ☺ ☺ ☹ ☺ ☺ ☹ ☺ ☺ ☺ ☹ ☺

❀ **Pleats** need to be ironed from the top to the bottom (see Figure 12-2). Hold the pleat down and iron the inside of the pleat first, and then iron over the outside.

❀ **Raised embroidery designs** can bunch up or pucker when ironing. Lay the fabric right-side down on top of a thick towel, and steam press with the appropriate setting for the fabric.

❀ **Seams,** especially on garments of a heavy fabric (such as wool), should be ironed on the inside first to flatten them. Then flip the garment over and iron the outside.

❀ **Sequined or beaded garments** should be ironed inside out on top of a plush towel. Use a pressing cloth and press with the iron on a gentle setting.

❀ **Shoulders of jackets or blouses** often bunch up and wrinkle near the seam when they're laid flat on the ironing board. Roll up a towel and push it up into the top of the sleeve near the shoulder seam. The towel provides a cushion so you can iron directly onto the seam and get a rounded edge.

❀ **Silk** is delicate and can be stained easily by a too-hot iron. Test the temperature of the iron on a hidden part of the garment first. Usually, a medium temperature iron is sufficient. To avoid any water spots or stains, set a steam iron on "no steam" or use a plain (non-steam) iron.

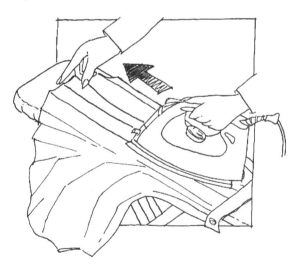

Figure 12-2: Ironing pleats.

☺ ☹ ☹ ☺ ☹ ☹ ☺ ☹ ☹ ☺ ☹ ☹ ☺ ☹ ☹ ☹ ☺ ☺ ☹ ☹ ☺

* **Ties** with slight wrinkles can be touched up by covering them with a handkerchief or cheesecloth and pressing lightly with a steam iron.

* **Velvet and corduroy** should be pressed inside out on top of a thick towel or on another piece of the same fabric. Use a light action and barely touch the back of the fabric.

* **Zippers** can sometimes pucker and refuse to lay flat. First, close the zipper and press the inside flaps. Then, open the zipper and press the surrounding fabric. Flip the fabric over to the right side and iron the outside fabric next to the opening.

Pressing matters for delicates

Pressing is different from ironing and is for delicate fabrics. To press properly, you move the iron up and down, lowering onto and lifting it up from the fabric rather than moving it back and forth. This up and down motion lets you smooth the fabric without any danger of stretching it. Naturally, pressing is the method of choice for delicate fabrics such as lace, wool, and napped, piled, or quilted textures. Place the fabric face down on a thick towel and press the wrong side of the fabric with a *steam iron* (that is, you set your iron to emit steam) on the appropriate setting.

A pressing cloth is a piece of fabric that's positioned between delicate fabric and the iron to protect the fabric from damage. You can use any piece of lightweight soft cloth: a men's handkerchief, a piece of lightweight muslin, cheesecloth, or an old cotton sheet.

Part 4

Home Maintenance 101

Sticking doors and pesky pests beware. This part covers home repairs and improvements. Look for quick projects, like hanging shelves and pictures on a wall, as well as a few more complicated projects, like replacing broken tile. You also find out where the power controls for your home's systems are so you can turn off a water main or flip a circuit breaker when necessary.

This part also shows you how to keep bugs out (out of your food, out of your house, and out of your life) in an environmentally friendly way. You also discover how to keep out intruders (human ones, that is) with a variety of safety measures, including deadbolts, motion sensitive lighting, and common sense.

Chapter **13**

Making Short Work of Basic Home Repairs

Go to any hardware store, and you'll be confronted by a myriad of tools for every task. What do you really need? That depends on the number and kind of home repairs you're going to do.

Even if you feel that you're all thumbs, every now and then, something in your home will stick, break, or flood with no repair person in sight. With a few simple household tools, you can conquer most minor repairs. This chapter helps you put together a basic tool kit and become comfortable with tools so you won't feel helpless when problems arise. It also helps you perform some of the most common household repairs.

Look Ma, No Tools: Quick-Fixers

Whether or not you can handle a hammer, the four following all-stars get you through many common household situations with ease:

❋ **Blue tack:** This reusable adhesive can hold lightweight pictures, posters, or decorations on walls without making a hole.

❋ **Duct tape:** Fix a leaking hose, repair pipe — the variety of repairs is endless.

❋ **Glue gun and glue sticks:** The tools of choice for decorators and home fixers — the glue dries super fast, and you can glue tons of stuff, from fabric to wood.

❋ **Staple gun and staples:** Basically, a staple gun is a very powerful stapler with a grip-and-lever handle. It works faster than nailing to attach carpeting to stairs, fabric to a headboard, or plastic sheeting to a window.

After you get used to these quick-fixers, you may never want to reach for a real tool again. Glue gun fanatics insist that everything should be glued instead of nailed, and staple-gun people are the same way. Experiment and you'll find plenty of uses for both.

Assembling a Basic Toolkit

For heavy-duty fixes, you need to keep a few tools on hand. Here are some tools that most home dwellers find useful:

- **Adjustable wrench:** Get an 8-inch size to handle most small- to medium-size nuts and bolts. Before buying, try adjusting the jaws to make sure they open and close smoothly.

- **Assorted nails, screws (bolts), nuts, and washers:** Keep in mind that nuts screw onto screws, and washers are placed between nuts and screws to lessen the chance of them coming unscrewed.

- **Claw hammer (13 or 16 ounces):** Smaller ones tend to be easier to hold and use, but test for yourself. Wood, steel, and fiberglass handles are available. Fiberglass is nice, because it's light and strong.

- **Crosscut saw:** Handy for cutting anything from plywood to paneling.

- **Files (wood and metal)**

- **³/₈-inch variable speed reversible drill:** Uses bits to drill holes and insert or remove screws.

- **Heavy-duty extension cord**

- **Plunger:** It's not a versatile tool but a real lifesaver when you need it.

- **Putty knife:** Get two: a 1-inch-wide one for filling cracks and holes and a 3-inch-wide one for larger openings.

- **Safety goggles:** Use when the repair involves hammering, splintering, or even painting overhead.

- **Sandpaper (fine to coarse grade)**

- **Screwdrivers:** The two basic types of screwdrivers are slotted and Phillips head. The *slotted screwdriver* has a single straight edge. The *Phillips screwdriver* has multiple edges in the form of a cross. Each type of screwdriver fits into its corresponding type of screws: single slot and Phillips. In general, you should have three different sizes of each type — large, small, and in-between.

- **Slip-joint pliers:** A wide variety of jaw sizes on this tool enables you to grip anything, including nails, nuts and bolts, and pipes.

☺ ☺ ☹ ☺ ☺ ☹ ☺ ☺ ☹ ☺ ☺ ☹ ☺ ☺ ☹ ☺ ☺ ☺ ☹ ☺

❊ **Tape measure:** A 25-foot retractable model with a metal tape and a thumb lock does the trick.

❊ **Utility knife or single edge razor blades**

For specialized tasks such as stripping floors, aerating your lawn, and so on, renting the tool you need will likely be most cost- and space-effective.

Solving Door Problems

Everyone has a sticking door, a squeaky door, or rattling door parts at one time or another. In this section, you find out how to keep your doors opening smoothly and soundlessly.

Unsticking doors

First, find out where the door is sticking. Look over the door carefully to check for any worn areas on the paint or finish. If you can't see anything, slip a piece of carbon paper on the top or bottom of the door frame and close the door on it to see where it rubs. If you don't have any carbon paper, use blackboard chalk to mark the areas.

If the door is tight on the hinge side, check to see if too much dried paint is preventing easy opening action. If so, strip or sand off some of the paint and then repaint it. If the door rubs on the floor, the problem may be loosening hinges. Check the hinge screws to make sure they're all tight. If they're loose, try replacing screws with ones that are about 1 1/2 times longer for a firmer hold. If that doesn't do the trick, hold a piece of coarse sandpaper beneath the door and move the door over it until it swings freely. If the door is tight on the jamb side, try coating the edge of the door with paraffin or a candle wax.

 Always fix a sticking door in cool, dry weather. Warmth and humidity swells wood, so the problem may be the weather, not the door.

Dealing with squeaks and rattles

To ease a squeak, lubricate the hinge and the hinge pin with a little household oil, like WD40, or with petroleum jelly.

Fix a rattley doorknob by tightening the tiny screws (called a *screw set*) in the front that holds the knob to its *spindle,* the metal shaft that runs through the door to hold both knobs in place. If that doesn't work, remove the doorknob and look at the spindle. If the spindle is bent, you'll have to replace it.

If a sliding door rattles or sticks, check the door *channels,* or guides, that are at the bottom (or, occasionally, the top) of the doorway. Replace them if they're worn or missing. If they aren't worn, try lubricating the channels with a graphite or silicone spray. Don't use oil; it will accumulate dirt.

Fixing Floors

If you have carpeting, wood, or linoleum flooring installed in your house, reserving extra yardage or setting aside sections of it for repairs is always a good practice — and you don't need bedroom-size portions, just linen closet size.

The following sections explain how to deal with various types of floor problems.

Replacing vinyl tiles

Remove old vinyl tile by doing the following:

1   **Place a towel over the tile and go over it with an iron set on low to loosen the adhesive (see Figure 13-1).**

Figure 13-1: Loosen the adhesive with a low iron.

2   **Use a putty knife to carefully pry up the tile without damaging those surrounding it.**

3   **Check to see that the new tile fits.**

If necessary, adjust the new tile to fit by sanding its edges with a fine-grade sandpaper.

4   **Vacuum the area to remove any dirt or debris, then apply new adhesive to the subfloor, as shown in Figure 13-2.**

Figure 13-2: Apply new adhesive to subfloor.

5   **Put the new tile in place and wipe off any excess adhesive.**

6   **Use a rolling pin on the tile to press it into place.**

Cover the pin with plastic wrap to make sure no glue gets on the rolling pin. Weigh down the tile with books or bricks for at least 8 hours. Figure 13-3 illustrates this process.

If you have a vinyl tile that's pulling away from the floor and curling up around the edges, place a towel over the tile and hold an iron on it long enough to soften the adhesive underneath. Lift up the tile and apply fresh adhesive to the curled area. Weigh down the tile with books or a brick until the adhesive dries.

☺ ☺ ☹ ☺ ☺ ☹ ☺ ☺ ☹ ☺ ☺ ☹ ☺ ☺ ☹ ☺ ☺ ☺ ☹ ☺

Figure 13-3: Replacing vinyl tiles.

Replacing ceramic tiles

Replacing a cracked or worn ceramic tile may seem stressful, but it's not really that hard. Just make sure that you wear safety glasses. Use a *cold chisel and hammer,* which is similar to a wood chisel, but its heavier steel is designed for cracking out masonry and old pipes.

1   **Start at the center of the tile and crack it out to the grout.**

2   **Remove the tile and the grout around it.**

3   **Vacuum out remaining pieces thoroughly.**

4   **Use a paint scraper and sandpaper to get up any remaining glue.**

    Remove any other debris.

5   **Apply tile adhesive and place in the new tile, centering it in the opening.**

6   **Let set overnight.**

☺ ☺ ☹ ☺ ☺ ☹ ☺ ☺ ☹ ☺ ☺ ☹ ☺ ☺ ☹ ☺ ☺ ☺ ☹ ☺

Follow grout instructions on a package of grout (being careful to match up the grout color to that of your current grout) to fill the area around the new tile.

Fixing squeaky floors

Squeaky floors may be caused by loose boards. Find the *joists* (supporting beams) that the flooring boards are attached to by locating the existing nail heads. Hammer 1¼-inch finishing nails or *brads* (another type of nail) through the flooring into the joists to stop the squeaks. Always try to fix a squeaky floor before installing any carpet. If a squeaky floor develops, lift up the carpet to hammer in the brads.

For a quick fix, try a lubricant like graphite. Sand some graphite from a pencil and work it into the cracks. A little talcum powder may also work. Wipe off the excess.

Fixing carpet problems

For immovable surface stains like glue spills or minor cigarette burns, try using a razor to gently shave the stain off the carpet surface.

If that doesn't do the trick, use that spare piece of carpeting you saved as a replacement. (If you don't have one or can't find it, cut away a small piece of carpet from a hidden area, such as inside a closet or under a piece of furniture that's never moved.)

The following instructions show you how to repair small stains using *double-face carpeting tape* (available at home centers or carpet stores), heavy-duty fabric glue, and a utility knife.

1 **Cut pieces of scrap carpeting slightly larger than the damaged spot.**

   To keep your cuts straight, use a metal ruler to guide the utility knife.

2 **Cut out the damaged area, using the cut piece of scrap carpeting as a template.**

   Be careful not to cut through the pad.

3 **Remove the damaged piece and put the new patch in place to make sure it fits.**

   Carefully trim it with scissors, if necessary. Then remove the patch.

149

4   **Put double-sided tape around the edges of the hole. Lightly apply fabric glue around the edges of the patch.**

5   **Lay the patch on the tape and press firmly in place to secure. Fluff up the fibers to make it match the surrounding area.**

Making Fast Furniture Repairs

Dressers, drawers, and side tables don't just hold your socks, T-shirts, and tea cups. They're also the proud holders of those little annoyances like sticky drawers and loose handles. But don't fret, for every problem, there's a solution.

Fixing sticky drawers

To repair a sticking drawer, first remove the drawer and check to see whether anything has come loose on the drawer or internally in the cabinet. Sometimes, you need to re-glue a loose side or tap the drawer back together with a hammer. Usually, it's the runners or *drawer channel glides* (internal supports that hold the drawer on both sides) that cause the problem. Rub the sides of the glides with a bar of soap or a piece of wax. Move the drawer back and forth in the cabinet to distribute the soap. If that doesn't work, try inserting two or three flat head thumbtacks toward the front on each drawer channel glide. They should do the trick.

Ironing out dents

Furniture gets bumped and dented — that's just the nature of life. Before resigning yourself to living with it forever, try ironing the dent away. Put your iron on a medium steam setting. Dampen several layers of clean cotton fabric, put them on the blemish, and let the iron sizzle away until it stops talking back. Repeat applications, if necessary, checking the surface after each one.

Tightening chair rungs

As soon as a chair starts to wobble, find the source. Usually, a *rung* (a piece of wood that runs between the legs of the chair) is beginning to work loose, which means that the glue is old and needs to be replaced. Work the rung loose all the way if you can. If that's not possible, dab around it with a cotton swab and a little warm vinegar to loosen the glue. Then pull out the rung.

To remove glue inside a round hole, wrap sandpaper around the end of a dowel or wooden spoon and insert it into hole. Or use your utility knife to scrape off all the old glue; be careful to take off just the glue, not the wood.

After you've scraped away all the glue, slip the rung into the hole. If it fits snugly, coat it with furniture glue and insert it in the socket. You don't want a loose fit. If the rung still appears loose, wrap some cotton thread around the end before you coat it with glue to make a tight fit.

To hold the chair together while the repaired rung is drying, wrap some twine around the two legs just below the rung and tie loosely. Then insert a couple of pencils into the twine and twist to tighten. You may want to wrap a soft, thick cloth around each leg first to prevent the rope from biting into the wood.

Dealing with loose knobs and pulls

If a knob or *pull* (that's a longer knob that screws into two holes) on furniture or a cabinet wiggles, the screw that secures the knob to the door or drawer is probably loose. Find it and tighten it.

If the knob is broken, you need to purchase a replacement, which is sometimes hard to match with what you already have. Consider giving your furniture a whole new look with new ceramic, metal, or wood knobs. Many decorative ones are available today at home centers. Just make sure that they fit in the old hole(s).

Working on Your Walls

Walls take a beating and call for frequent intervention. The following sections describe ways to manage the most common problems.

Sealing small holes

To seal a small hole, you need to apply some ready-mix spackle. You can purchase a small container of it at a home center store.

To fix the hole, do the following:

1 **Brush away any loose material or cracked edges.**

   Moistening the area with a damp sponge sometimes helps, but check the instructions on your spackle first.

2 **Use your finger or a putty knife to apply the spackle into the hole.**

3 Let it dry and then sand it smooth with a fine-grade sandpaper.

After you finish, reseal the spackle tub tightly because it dries out quickly.

For larger holes, repeat the process. It may take several applications, but the end result is definitely worthwhile.

Repairing ripped wallcovering

If a piece of wallcovering gets ripped or torn, always try to repair what's there first. You may be able to rub the back of the tear with some latex adhesive and smooth it into place.

If you can't repair the tear with what remains, you'll have to patch it. Ideally, when you wallpaper you should save any remnants left over from a roll, which you can later use for repairs. If no remnants or new rolls are available, remove some wallcovering from an inconspicuous area — behind a dresser, for example — to make a patch.

1 Cut a piece of covering to match the pattern, making sure it is slightly larger than the damaged area.

2 Hold the piece against the wall, lightly taping it into place if necessary.

3 Cut through both layers of the covering with a sharp utility knife.

If possible, follow any vertical or horizontal lines in your pattern, which will help hide the cut edges.

4 Remove the damaged area and fit the new patch in place, securing it with adhesive.

 Depending on where the damage is, this may be the perfect time and place to hang a picture over the damaged spot.

Hanging items on the wall

Hanging pictures is one project that practically everyone has to cope with at one time or another. Consider the weight and size of the item you're dealing with and the kind of wall you're hanging it on. Put your item on the bathroom scale to get an exact weight and use a tape measure to find out exact dimensions. Take these measurements with you to the hardware store.

You can choose from many different types of hangers and hooks available for practically every hanging situation. The instructions on the back of the hanger/hook package tell you which one to choose.

Hanging lightweight items

To hang an item that weighs 10 pounds or less, you can use prepackaged picture hooks and nails or the adhesive hangers on plaster and drywall. For something a little heavier, two hooks nailed at about two-thirds the width of the frame give it extra support and prevent it from shifting.

To prevent damage to the wall surface, you may want to use a fastener called an *anchor*, which helps prevent chipping and is especially helpful in plaster and cement walls.

You drill a hole slightly smaller than the anchor (see the recommended drill size on the package). Then hammer the anchor into the wall. When you insert the screw, it opens up the anchor, hooking it into the wall for a more secure grip.

Hanging medium to heavyweight items

To hang objects that weigh 20 pounds or more in hollow walls, consider using toggle bolts or expansion bolts.

Toggle bolts have spider-like legs that open and snug up to the inside of the wall. To use, you drill a hole big enough for the bolt to fit into. Then you take off the screw and put it through the hanger on your frame or shelf. Reattach the toggle and push the toggle assembly back into the wall and tighten the screw (see Figure 13-4).

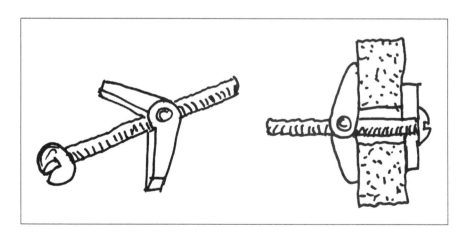

Figure 13-4: A toggle bolt.

Expansion bolts, or molly bolts (also called *mollies*), shown in Figure 13-5, are a combination anchor and toggle bolt. They open up, securing the housing inside the wall and gripping it. They won't fall off when you remove the screw the way toggle bolts do, so you can change what you're hanging. They also come in a variety of wall widths. To use, drill a hole for the bolt to fit, put the molly inside, and turn the screw until it flattens against the wall. If you're hanging something weighing 30 pounds or more, use at least two mollies to distribute the weight more evenly.

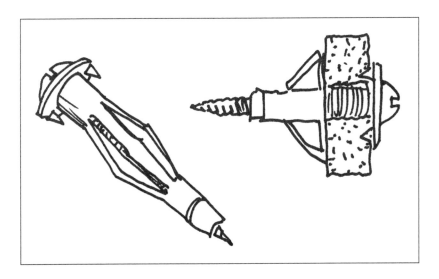

Figure 13-5: Expansion or molly bolts.

Finding studs

Very heavy items are best nailed into the *studs*, the vertical beams in the wall. Studs are usually 16 inches apart but in some new construction can be as much as 24 inches apart. Most of the time, studs are wood, but some modern high rise apartments have steel. If you're going to be doing a lot of hanging, you may want to buy a *stud finder,* an electronic device that signals when it passes over a stud.

Other ways of finding a stud are to knock lightly on the wall with your fist in a horizontal direction. The wall will sound hollow until you reach the more solid tones of the stud. Or check the baseboards for nail heads that are usually driven into the studs.

Chapter 14

Bugs, Be Gone!

Nothing is creepier than spotting an army of pests marching across your floor, and if you see one bug, you gotta know that more are around. They're entering your house from some hidden place, and they're up to no good.

Remember that the best offense is a good defense. Mount your defensive strategy immediately:

❁ **Lock out bugs.** Screens (without rips and tears) should be every-where — not just on the windows, but covering any opening: the chimney, vents, and shower and bath drains. Inspect the outside of your house for any cracks or crevices where varmints can enter. Look for openings around the telephone, cable, and electrical wires that enter the house. Seal any openings with caulk.

❁ **Cut down on their water supply.** Pipes, faucets, toilets, bathtubs, and washing machines provide much-needed drink for any thirsty critter. Check under sinks in the bathroom and kitchen, and check the laundry area for dripping pipes and faucets or for standing water. Regularly pull out and empty the drip pan under the refrigerator

❁ **Stop feeding them.** Don't ever leave food sitting around unpro-tected. Store food supplies in tightly sealed glass or plastic contain-ers. Wash dishes, including pet food bowls, immediately after each meal. If you want to leave a pot or pan soaking in the sink, fill it with soapy water and wash it before you go to bed. Make sure your garbage can is covered with a tight-fitting lid.

If bugs do invade your home, you also need to go on the offensive. For yourself and your environment, when you see or suspect pests, first try the following nontoxic bug beaters. Some of these products will be on the shelves right in your kitchen; you'll find others in your neighborhood garden center.

- **Soap:** Mix together 1 tablespoon of liquid dishwashing soap in a quart of water. Spray it on the bugs or set it around in saucers. When the bugs search for water, they lap up the soap, and it's curtains for them! Because this soapy solution is so mild, you may need to reapply it every few days.

- **Diatomaceous earth:** Diatomaceous (dye-at-oh-MAY-shuss) earth is a horticultural-grade mineral dust, available in garden centers, that kills insects without affecting animals, birds, or people. Mix this mineral dust with water and spray it on plants or sprinkle it around a garden as a bug barrier.

- **Pyrethrum:** This pesticide, made from the blossoms of dried pyrethrum (pie-WREATH-rum) plants (a daisy-like type of chrysanthemum), is an effective insecticide against many bugs, from roaches to termites to white flies. It works fast and is not harmful to humans.

Combating Kitchen Critters

It makes sense that bugs would love to join your snacking in the kitchen. Many of them love to eat the grains and dried foods that you store on your shelves.

Two of the most commonly seen kitchen bugs are

- **Meal moths:** You can sometimes see meal moths flying around at night. You can tell they've been in the food because they leave little threads that clump together with the food on the sides of the package.

- **Flour beetles:** These bugs lay eggs in bags of flour; the eggs become covered with flour and stick on the side of the container.

Some classic methods of repelling these prolific bugs include sprinkling bay leaves in the storage containers or spreading them on kitchen shelves. Another kitchen spice — black pepper — not only repels but also kills the bugs.

 Inspect all boxes and bags of food before you bring them home from the store. Look for holes in the bag or clumps that cling to the side. To be extra cautious, transfer bug-free food to metal, glass, or heavy plastic containers with tight-fitting lids, preferably with a rubber seal.

If you do find bugs on your shelves, remove whatever food they're in and throw the food away. Check everything else around it to make sure the bugs haven't moved on to their next course in the next-door box or bag. Remove any infested food and wash the area with a heavy-duty household cleaner.

Attacking ants

One thing ants don't like is a clean kitchen. Keep your kitchen clean, and the ants will be put off. Minimally, do these three basic tasks:

❀ Always wash the dishes after meals and wipe off counters.

❀ Clean off jars that contain sticky or oily substances that drip — such as honey, corn syrup, or maple syrup.

❀ Sponge down the counter with a cloth soaked in vinegar or spray the surfaces with citrus oil and water — both are smells that ants don't like.

Use any of the following methods to keep ants out of the house:

❀ Plant peppermint at your entrances. You can also crush mint leaves and sprinkle them around the door.

❀ Place coffee grounds around the doors and windows where they enter.

❀ Follow the ants back to where they entered the home and make a solid line about ¹/₄-inch wide with cayenne pepper, turmeric, powdered charcoal, and powdered cleanser containing chlorine bleach. They won't want to cross the barrier.

If you develop a problem with ants indoors, spritz the ants with a household-cleaning product such as window cleaner or household spray like Formula 409. Or use a mixture of 1 teaspoon liquid dishwashing soap and water in a spray bottle. If you spot some tiny cracks around windowsills, baseboards, and thresholds, cover them with petroleum jelly temporarily, but caulk them as soon as you can.

Buzzing off the lowly fly

Flies are more than just annoying; they also carry plenty of germs with them. Many diseases, from hepatitis to cholera, have been attributed to the fly. Hit them with a fly swatter or a rolled up piece of paper or magazine.

If you can't catch the fly, spray it with a little hair spray, spray starch, or rubbing alcohol to stun them and slow down their buzzing enough for you to land a punch. The following natural repellents are also quite good for warding off flies:

❀ Put sweet clover from your front yard in little bags of netting (you can buy the fabric in a fabric or camping store) and hang above doorways in your house.

☺ ☺ ☹ ☺ ☺ ☹ ☺ ☺ ☹ ☺ ☺ ☹ ☺ ☺ ☹ ☺ ☺ ☺ ☹ ☺

❁ Make a potpourri from bay leaves, cloves, eucalyptus leaves, and clover blossoms. Crush slightly to release the scent and hang in netting bags.

❁ Outside of the house, a few basil or tansy plants around your doorways keeps flies away.

Avoid using pest strips or aerosol pesticides, which emit toxic vapors that can get into your lungs.

Flies like garbage and food. So keep the fly population down with good cleaning habits.

❁ Don't leave food out on the kitchen counters.

❁ Hose down garbage cans after they're empty, dry them thoroughly, and sprinkle the bottoms with dry soap. Always keep the lids on and repair or replace them if they get any cracks or holes.

❁ Separate your wet and dry garbage if possible. Wrap anything that's soggy with several layers of newspaper.

❁ Rinse out bottles and cans that you're saving for recycling.

Getting rid of roaches

The roach problem is one of the most common and most repulsive for homeowners. Roaches are especially prevalent in older houses and apartment buildings.

If you suspect that you have a roach problem — but aren't sure where they're coming from — you need to find out where the little critters are hiding. Outsmart them by turning off the lights and shining a flashlight on the areas where you think they might be lurking. You'll see them go scattering about.

Periodically, give appliances a thorough check by pulling them out and cleaning the area behind and underneath. If you see signs of roaches, vacuum up droppings from the floor and wash the area thoroughly with a strong household cleanser. Throw away the vacuum cleaner bag afterward.

Checking into the roach motel

One of the simplest solutions is to put out *roach motels,* which you can buy at any home store. The insides of roach motels are coated with sticky stuff, and when bugs step inside the boxes, their feet get stuck and they can't move. Put the roach motels around the baseboards and walls in the kitchen, bathroom, and any other place you think roaches might hang out. Check

the motels frequently and keep track of how many get caught in the trap. You'll be able to see which areas of your home need more serious help.

Using boric acid as bait

The best way to get rid of roaches is boric acid. It's very effective, and it's better for the environment than more toxic pesticides because it doesn't evaporate into the air. Be sure to get the kind that's rated 99 percent pure acid, which is more effective than other kinds.

You have to be cautious, because boric acid can be toxic if ingested. Always keep it out of the reach of small children and pets. When you apply it to infested areas, don't let it get on your skin or breathe it in. Put on a mask and gloves and wear a long-sleeved shirt and long pants to avoid exposing any skin.

To apply, sprinkle, spray, or use it as bait directly on surfaces where roaches live so they'll scamper through it. Here's how:

* **Sprinkling boric acid around:** When you sprinkle it around, the roaches walk in it and ingest it. Put it along the edges of base-boards, in corners, and under appliances. Spread the acid around evenly where they gather — just dumping it in blobs won't be effec-tive because they will figure out how to travel around it. Use a bulb duster or turkey baster to gently blow it into small crevices, base-boards, and under walls and sinks. Of course, never use that turkey baster for food preparation again.

* **Spraying boric acid:** Mix a light solution of 1 teaspoon boric acid to 1 quart water and shake well. Spray it in the crevices, base-boards, or dark corners where roaches lurk. Reapply as necessary. Be careful not to spray it where kids or pets can get into it.

* **Making a bait:** If you'd rather make up a yummy bait that the roaches will eat, mix together 1/2 cup borax (another form of boric acid), 1/4 cup flour, 1/4 cup cornmeal, 1/8 cup powdered sugar. Sprinkle the mixture onto plastic lids or paper plates and let it sit for about 10 days. Repeat if roaches are still around. Be sure you place this mixture in areas where children or pets can't get to it because it is poisonous if eaten.

Commercial bait traps, such as Combat, are also effective and very safe because they are self-contained. They may be good to use if small children and pets are running around the house.

Fighting Other Household Bugs

Bugs make their way into other rooms of the house in search of warm and cozy hideouts and a fresh food supply. Sometimes, they're annoying

hitchhikers on your favorite pet; other times, they seek out and destroy your prized possessions, including your wardrobe. Whatever your situation, read on for tips to combat the tiny armies.

Fighting fleas

Fleas can make the lives of both you and your pet miserable. Not only do they ride in on your animal's fur, but they can jump off and hide in the furniture and carpet. Fleas love the warm, humid temperatures of late summer and fall, so the problem escalates at that time of year. If your pet has fleas, tiny black dots show up on its grooming comb that you can get at any pet store; when you shake the dots onto the light colored paper, they turn red. Comb your pet often to pick up fleas and eggs on its fur. Then dip the comb in a mixture of rubbing alcohol and water to kill the fleas.

The best way to keep fleas off your pet is constant grooming and cleaning. Bathe your pet often and give him a thorough shampooing with a mild soap or flea shampoo. Rub the soap all over your pet's body, literally from head to tail. Let the shampoo sit on his skin for about five minutes to drown the fleas. Always groom your pet outdoors if you think he has fleas, in order to keep them from infesting the house.

Check with your vet to see whether she recommends any of the topically applied flea treatments and prevention aides currently available. Medication like Frontline and Advantage are commercially available for both cats and dogs. They break the fleas' lifecycle immediately, making the problem much easier to manage.

 If you prefer to go the natural route, you can make your own flea-repelling potion with simple ingredients you have around the house. Cut up three lemons and put them in a bowl with 3 cups of boiling water. Let the mixture steep overnight and sponge this mixture over your pet's skin. The fleas should die immediately.

Even though you clean your pet, you could still have fleas lingering around the house. Vacuum all carpets, upholstered furniture, and floors every few days to keep down the fleas. Throw away the vacuum bag afterward to avoid reintroducing fleas when you vacuum next.

If you have a real problem, you may need to sprinkle your carpet with a flea-treating borate powder. Check with your pet supply store for specific brands. Rub the powder evenly into the carpet and then vacuum, following the instructions on the box. To avoid breathing in the powder, wear a dust mask and goggles while you apply this mixture.

Conquering clothes moths

You can usually see the telltale signs of moths or carpet beetles when you take your clothes out of storage for the season. After moths have chomped on your clothing, you can see holes with jagged edges.

Cedar closets have long been used to repel, but most people don't have the luxury of a cedar-lined closet. However, you can buy cedar planks and paneling at home centers to install on the walls of an existing closet. Cedar coat hangers and chips or small hanging balls of cedar have some repelling qualities, but they aren't as effective as lining an entire closet.

Another moth-control method is to tie a few bay leaves together and hang them from the closet rod. Or make herbal sachets by wrapping a combination of lavender, mint, cloves, eucalyptus, or black pepper in a square of loose fabric or netting. Experiment to see what scents you like best. Just remember to squeeze the herbs from time to time to release the scent.

Vacuum closets regularly to remove hair, lint, or insects. If you see signs of infestation, remove everything from the closet. Then check for damage and throw away anything that's been attacked. Dry clean or wash the rest of your clothes. Recheck regularly, because you can easily miss moth eggs or the moths themselves.

Sinking the silverfish

Silverfish (those tiny, almost translucent, worm-like critters that may scurry about your bathroom) love areas with high humidity and usually move at night, eating the glue in book bindings and wallpaper and the paste on stamps, to name a few favorites.

If you find silverfish in books, clear off the shelves and vacuum both the books and the shelves. Dust shelves, cracks, and crevices with boric acid, diatomaceous earth, or Epsom salts. If you're putting books away for long-term storage, sprinkle some boric acid around the container to keep silverfish out. With all these treatments, avoid areas that are accessible to animals or young children and wear goggles and a mask while applying. A safer but less effective alternative is to sprinkle the shelves with cloves.

Make a silverfish trap by wrapping a glass jar with strips of masking tape from top to bottom. This creates a rough surface for the bugs to climb on. Mix a little flour and sugar and put it in the bottom of the jar. Place the trap near the area where you've found silverfish. The bugs will be attracted to the food and climb in, but they won't be able to climb out. Check the trap each day. If you trap any silverfish, clean them out and replace the food.

Keeping spiders in check

Remember *Charlotte's Web?* Well, spiders are your friends, they help keep other pests under control. Most spiders are harmless, just not too pleasant to look at.

If you see spider webs in your house, brush them away with a broom covered with an old T-shirt. If any spiders fall down, crush them with your foot. Keep the whole house clean by frequently vacuuming their hiding places, which are along baseboards and moldings and inside closets. Keep the outside of the house clean, too. Trim bushes and trees so the branches aren't hanging over the house. Don't let leaves pile up near the house and under shrubs and trees. Inspect your gutters frequently and remove any leaves that have accumulated.

To keep spiders from entering the house, soak a few cotton balls in rubbing alcohol and put them where you think the spiders are coming into the house.

Keeping Track of Your Pest Management

Keep track of your pests, problem areas, and treatment schedule with Table 14-1, listing what pests you find in various locations, what treatment you've used on which date, and when you plan to recheck.

Table 14-1 Tracking Your Pesky Pests

Pest	Location	Treatment	Date	Recheck Date

Chapter 15

A Safe Home Is a Safe Haven

If you're like many families, you spend a lot of time in your home, and you want your family to feel safe and secure at all times. Many people think an alarm system and a deadbolt are the only elements to maintaining a safe home, but you have many other safety issues to consider, including food safety and being prepared for emergencies. In this chapter, I give you some tips for keep your home and family safe from outside and inside invaders.

Avoiding Home Safety Hazards

Keeping safe from hazards inside the home is as important as protecting yourself and your family from outside intruders. The following safety tips help prevent fires and other disasters:

❀ **Make sure extension cords are in good condition and aren't worn or damaged.** If the cord feels hot while you're using it, unplug and discard it. If an outlet or switch is hot to the touch, don't turn it on. Call an electrician to check it.

❀ **Dry your hands before using or plugging and unplugging an appliance.** Stay away from water when using any electrical tool.

❀ **If an electrical appliance falls into the tub, sink, or pool, don't reach into the water to get it, even if it is turned off.** Unplug it first. It can electrocute anyone who touches the water or who is in the water. Have an electrician install ground fault circuit interrupters in any outlet in a wet or damp environment, like the kitchen, bathroom, basement, or garage. GFCIs shut off power if they sense a short in the circuit from an appliance or tool, preventing electric shock when a plugged-in appliance falls in water.

☺ ☺ ☹ ☺ ☺ ☹ ☺ ☺ ☹ ☺ ☺ ☹ ☺ ☺ ☹ ☺ ☺ ☹ ☺

❋ **Don't remove the grounding prong on a three-prong plug.** If you only have two pronged outlets in your house, get an adapter with a ground tab.

❋ **Unplug small appliances when you're not using them and when you go away on vacation.** That way, if these short out when you're gone, a fire won't start. Never use an extension cord for major appliances or for heat-producing appliances, such as a portable heater or iron. Always unplug appliances before repairing them.

Also remember to always keep a fire extinguisher handy in all or most rooms of your house. Your initial investment will pay off in the long run.

Food Safety

Even if you eat out often, you still eat at home at least part of the time. You can ensure the safety of the food you serve and prepare your family by buying fresh foods and handling them properly. Watch for "sell-by" and expiration days on everything from eggs, milk, and fresh meats to canned goods and boxed dinners. If you're running other errands before going home, keep a cooler or heavy-duty insulated bag in your car to keep cold items cold. After you get your food home from the grocery store, put all refrigerator and freezer items away immediately.

Washing hands

Always wash your hands for at least 20 seconds with warm water and soap before and after you prepare food. If you're interrupted while preparing food, wash your hands before you stop to do something else. This prevents you from spreading any bacteria onto any other surface you may happen to touch, like the cabinet doors, the countertop, and a knife handle.

Thawing food safely

Don't thaw frozen meat, poultry, or seafood at room temperature. It may feel cold to the touch, but bacteria can still multiply. Choose one of these three easy and safe methods:

❋ **Defrost in the refrigerator.** Always set the meat on a plate to prevent juices from leaking onto other foods.

❋ **Defrost in the microwave.** Cook the food immediately after defrosting.

❋ **Defrost in a plastic bag in a pan filled with cold water.** Change water every 30 minutes.

Cooking food correctly

Health experts suggest that you thoroughly cook meat, poultry, and fish as well as dishes with eggs to kill harmful bacteria. Use a quick-read meat thermometer to give an accurate reading. Place the thermometer at the thickest portion of the meat away from the bone. Avoid interrupted cooking: Don't cook food partially ahead of time, store it, then finish grilling or roasting it later.

Follow these temperature guidelines from the USDA for determining when food is thoroughly cooked:

* **Cook ground meat** to 160°

* **Cook ground poultry** to 165°

* **Cook beef, veal, lamb steaks, roast, and chops** to 145°

* **Cook fresh pork** to 160°

* **Cook whole poultry** to 180° for dark meat and 170° for white.

Putting Security First

Security is an important issue, especially when you have a family. You're no longer just protecting yourself; you're protecting your kids. Think like a burglar and put as many obstacles in their way as you make your home less of a target.

Teaching your kids to be safe

Have a family meeting and tell them what you think is proper behavior. Most kids have a tendency to tell everything about themselves and their families. Explain to them that they shouldn't give out any vital information to strangers. For example, when they answer the telephone, instruct them to tell the caller that "My mother can't come to the phone right now," rather than "My mother's at work and won't be home for hours."

Make sure you teach your children how to dial 911 in case of an emergency. Always leave a list of emergency numbers by the phone, as well as your street address written down. People – especially kids – often forget their addressees in an emergency. Or help your kids call out by getting a programmable phone so they have to know only how to punch in simple numbers. If you have baby-sitters, give them the list of emergency numbers and a number where you can always be reached. (Your home address and phone number written out prominently is good for sitters, too.)

Lighten up

Good lighting can make you look good and your house look bad to burglars. Besides acting as a safety device, lighting can also create a stage-like setting that burglars will be wary of performing on. Because lighting is unattractive to burglars, use it as a deterrent to intimidate intruders.

Illuminate as large an area as possible with the lowest level of lights. Use two lights around your front door, if possible, so if one burns out, one still remains to light the way. Here are some other ways to use lighting to make your home more safe:

- **Install infrared detectors to your existing lighting, front steps, path, or floodlights so that they light up when someone passes by them.** They come on only when needed so you save energy and fool intruders into thinking they've been spotted.

- **Use a time clock device to activate your outdoor lights.** But don't forget to adjust it for Daylight Savings Time.

- Have your address well lit so emergency crews or the police can find your house quickly.

Secure windows and doors

Walk around your house and think like a burglar. Test every entrance for easy entry, keeping track of what you find on Table 15-2. See Table 15-1 for an example

Table 15-1 Sample Entrance Security Inventory

Entrance	Device	Replace/Upgrade?	Date
Front Door	Deadbolt	No	2/18/04
Basement window	Lock	Yes—replace lock	2/18/04

Table 15-2 My Entrance Security Inventory

Entrance	Device	Replace/Upgrade?	Date

Use the following tips to make sure your doors and windows are protecting you as they should.

❀ **Make sure every outside entrance door has a dead bolt lock in addition to its doorknob lock.** A dead bolt is installed separately from the door knob lock; when its key is turned to the locked position, a strong metal bolt slides at least an inch into a metal box called a *strike plate* on the frame of the door.

❀ **Replace flimsy exterior doors with solid ones.** Outside doors should be *solid core* (not hollow) and at least 1 ³/₄ inches thick. Avoid *hollow-core doors;* these are hollow inside and can be easily kicked in.

❀ **Check that your entrance and exit doors open in, not out, so that the hinges are on the inside and can't be removed.** If your door swings out, put in metal door pins that mount into the side of a door and go into a hole in the door frame as the door closes. This prevents someone from removing the hinge pins and lifting out the door. You may need to hire some help for this.

❀ **Check your patio or sliding doors and install a security bar and sturdy lock.** You can also purchase a bar with special lights and an alarm.

❀ **Make a daily or weekly check to see whether windows are secure.** Double-check and lock them before you leave the house.

Follow security do's and don'ts

No super-duper security system or titanium bolt on your door can make up for leaving your door unlocked. The best defense is usually common sense. Here are a few do's and don'ts:

Do's

Do the following to prepare for or follow up on a break-in:

❀ **Do have an escape plan in case you hear an intruder.** Get out of the house quickly and call the police from a neighbor's house.

❀ **Do make a written inventory of all your possessions along with pictures of the valuable items.** Or make a videotape of your possessions, describing each item and what it's worth. Keep these in a safe place like a safety deposit box.

❀ **Do buy home insurance.** Check with a reputable company or agent for the proper amount of protection.

❀ **Do call the police immediately** if you discover your house has been broken into or robbed.

- **Do keep a phone by your bed** with a number programmed for the police department.

- **Do secure your home, but don't oversecure it.** In case of a fire, make sure you can easily get out of the house. Everyone in the house should be aware of escape routes and the locations of keys for locks or bars over doors and windows.

- **Do have separate car and house keys.** A parking valet could make a copy of your house keys and "visit" your home later. And if you do get carjacked, the thief has only your car keys, not your house keys, too.

Don'ts

Try to avoid trouble by following these tips:

- **Don't confront a burglar.** And don't tip-toe around if you hear an intruder. Let them know you're there by shouting that you're calling the police. If you're alone, pretend other family members are around.

- **Don't put your name on the mailbox.** Just list the house number. And avoid listing your full name in the phone book. List yourself by the last name or with an initial.

- **Don't include your address in classified ads.** If strangers come to your house to buy something, have friends there.

- **Don't let anyone in your house whom you don't know and aren't expecting;** always ask for proper identification. Don't be intimidated. If you feel unsafe, you probably are.

- **Don't go in your house if you come home to an opened door and things look amiss.** Go to a neighbor's house and call the police.

Ten Childproofing Tips

❋ **Install childproof latches on cabinets, drawers, and doors.**
Use these latches to secure glassware, chemicals, spices, knives, matches, plastic bags, and anything that needs to be kept from kids.

❋ **Move anything potentially dangers to a high shelf or cabinet.**
Anything from chemicals to knickknacks to knitting needles can be a hazard for children. Keep temptation out of sight and reach.

❋ **Scour your bathroom for items that can cause cuts or scratches.**
Do this regularly to ensure that razors aren't left on the edge of a tub or that nail scissors or tweezers aren't on a counter where kids may play with them.

❋ **Never leave your child alone in the tub or near the toilet.**
A child can drown in either. Consider installing a locking lid.

❋ **Use the stove's back burners and keep pot handles turned toward the back of the stove.**
If you're in the market for a new stove, look for one with the controls on the back of the stove rather than the front.

❋ **Anchor dressers, shelving units, and armoires to the wall.**
An unsecured dresser can topple on a climbing child.

❋ **Keep small unsupervised children out of the bathroom.**
Buy sliding door knob covers or install simple hook and eye closures out of reach of toddlers.

❋ **Keep all cords away from children.**
Children can get tangled in phone, electrical, and window-treatment cords. They can quickly injure themselves.

❋ **Don't lay your baby down to sleep on your bed.**
The child can roll off or suffocate in any soft comforters or pillows.

❋ **Before you bathe your child, test the water temperature.**
Wrists are more sensitive to hot water than fingers, so test what's too hot for babies skin by placing a few drops there.

Ten Quick Cleaning Tasks

❀ **Clean out a junk drawer.**
Dump everything in your drawer into an empty box and go through the stuff. Throw away old batteries, no-name keys, and other unneeded junk. Organize and replace the remaining items.

❀ **Update your address book.**
Cross out, erase, or otherwise remove any names or numbers that are outdated. Update records for people who have recently moved.

❀ **Clean the front of the refrigerator.**
First remove the magnets holding schedules, works of art, and photos. File or toss what's outdated, wash the front of the fridge, and replace much-loved and oft-used items with magnets.

❀ **Straighten your desk.**
Pick up each piece of paper, and then either file it or throw it away. Put pens, your stapler, scissors, and other items in their places.

❀ **Change the bed sheets.**
If you keep a second set of sheets clean and ready to use, this task takes just a few minutes. Wash the dirty sheets the next time you do laundry, so that a clean set is ready for your next change of sheets.

❀ **Hand-wash some clothes.**
It's not as hard as you may think. (See Chapter 11 for suggestions.)

❀ **Clean out your purse or briefcase.**
Sit on a floor with a wastebasket nearby and pour out everything in the purse or briefcase. Throw away any trash or unneeded items and organize the remaining contents.

❀ **Straighten out the medicine cabinet.**
Throw out expired medicines, rusty razor blades, makeup more than six months old, and so on. Wipe off the shelves.

❀ **Reduce your junk mail.**
Send a postcard with your name and address to Mail Preference Service, P.O. Box 9008, Farmington, NY 11735-9008.

❀ **Sweep or vacuum one room.**
A clean sweep or fresh vacuuming works wonders for a room. See Chapter 8.

Index

Index

☺ ☺ ☹ ☺ ☺ ☹ ☺ ☺ ☹ ☺ ☺ ☹ ☺ ☺ ☹ ☺ ☺ ☺ ☹ ☺

Index

Index

☺ ☹ ☹ ☺ ☹ ☹ ☺ ☹ ☹ ☺ ☹ ☹ ☺ ☹ ☹ ☹ ☺ ☺ ☹ ☹ ☺

Look for all The Parent's Success Guide™ titles at your local Target® store.

The Parent's Success Guide™